A GUIDE FOR PARENTS

PRESERVING A RIGHTEOUS SEED

JOYCE THOMPSON

Copyright© 1998 by Joyce Thompson.
All rights reserved. No part of this book may be reproduced in any form whatever, except for brief quotations, without the written permission of the publisher:

        CTM Publishing
        P.O. Box 763954
        Dallas, Texas 75376-3954

All biblical Scriptures are taken from the New American Standard Bible, compiled and edited by Frank Charles Thompson, D.D., Ph.D., B.B. Kirkbride Bible Co., Inc., Indianapolis, Indiana, USA (1993).

All dictionary definitions are from the *Reader's Digest O:iford Complete Wordfinder,* published by the Reader's Digest Association, Inc., Pleasantville, NY, 10570, Oxford University Press, Inc., (1996).

ISBN# 1-879655-04-7

Dedication

To my wonderful sons, Victor, Steven, Jason and Joseph. May you each be instruments of God's righteousness, helping extend His glory as it covers the earth.

Contents

Acknowledgments	4
Introduction	5

CHAPTER

1.	Where God Is There Is Order	7
2.	Order in the Home	13
3.	The Importance of Fathers	17
4.	Satan Has a Plan for Your Child	29
5.	"Stuff" on the Hard Drive (Disk)	33
6.	Dealing With Rebellion	35
7.	Kids are Like Race Horses	43
8.	Pain is a Necessary Part of Life	49
9.	Important Concepts in Rearing Children	61
10.	False Concepts Under Which We Rear Our Children	77
11.	Concepts That Destroy Order in the Home	91
12.	Teen Suicide and Violence	101

Resource Suggestions	114

Acknowledgments

While writing this book, I have interviewed a number of people who are outstanding in the field of education, others who have reared wonderful children, and those who have worked with children and young people extensively.

Special thanks to Carrol Thompson, my husband, best friend, and teacher.

My thanks to Victor Thompson, our eldest son; Pam Thompson and Carol Ann Perry, outstanding, award-winning teachers; Carl and Alice Nine, educators, exceptional parents, grandparents, and pastors; Laurel Sabin, who has a doctorate in special education; Dottie Jones, mentor, counselor, and volunteer chaplain in the Texas Department of Criminal Justice.

And thanks to outstanding parents: Ron and Carol Keller, parents of eight children; David and Wanda Alldredge, parents of three children; Warren and Sheril Stevens from Australia, parents of four children; and last, but not least, my own parents who lived godly lives of peace, order, and compatibility. They were married 63 years, and I never saw them fight or quarrel.

Cover Artist: Jonathan Biddlecombe

Introduction

Rearing children is the most important thing you will ever do in your life. It is nothing less than an opportunity to actively participate in God's redemptive plan. Few parents understand the great privilege it represents or the magnitude of their responsibility before God.

Throughout the Bible, God has conveyed His desire to establish an order that would bring about a righteous seed. He could have lived for Himself, and skipped the pain of loving rebellious children but instead, He chose the role of a father.

God sent Jesus, His only begotten Son, to earth to shed His righteous blood that He might gain other sons and daughters and leave a pattern of life for us to follow.

Our goal as Christian parents is to duplicate His righteous life for our children that they might be prepared to choose God's will and God's ways for their lives.

The problem is that childrearing can be a slippery slope. I know because I have raised four sons and two daughters of my own. It is easy to feel overwhelmed and intimidated. In the early churches, there were special benches for women who were widows with grown children. This was possibly a place of honor, but more than that, it was probably intended to identify the women who were qualified to give advice to the younger women because of their experience.

Though we do not have benches set aside for such women in our churches today, there remains a great need for the wisdom and encouragement of those who have traveled the road ahead and are now able to provide guidelines to help along the way. Experience counts!

I hope you will find in these pages the wisdom and encouragement you need to accomplish your parenting task. All that needs to be said on the subject would hardly fit into one book, and I have not tried to cover everything. My focus has been on the place righteousness should have in rearing children. I believe it will be helpful to you as you set out to raise sons and daughters who are pleasing to the Lord.

Remember that you are more than just a mother-more than just a father. God has made you a vital link in His eternal plan.

Chapter One

Where God Is There Is Order

God lives in an order of righteousness, which means He lives in an order that is morally right, virtuous, law abiding, ethical, good, honest, just, fair, and trustworthy. Consider the following:

> God lives in purity, where there is no mixture of good and evil.
>
> God lives in perfection, where there are no flaws or blemishes.
>
> God lives in fullness, where there is no lack.
>
> God lives in eternal life, where there is no death.
>
> God lives in faithfulness, compassion, kindness, grace and mercy.

It is the nature and work of righteousness to establish order, and it is His will and purpose to bring us, as His children, into that order where He lives.

> I Peter 1: 14-16 says: *As obedient children, do not be conformed to the former lusts which were yours in your ignorance, but like the Holy One who called you, be holy yourselves also in all your behavior; because it is written, 'You shall be holy, for I am Holy.'*

What does God mean when He says "be holy"? The word *holy*

means morally and spiritually excellent or perfect. Holiness is God's essence (core of being), the inherent, permanent characteristics and nature of Who He is. He is saying, "I want you to be morally and spiritually excellent also."

As Christians, holiness must be our nature, the very essence of who we are, because God Himself has commanded us to be holy. It must, therefore, be possible since God Himself mandates it. Most Christians are so spiritually weak, they don't see holiness even as a possibility.

The word most often used to express this holiness is righteousness. This is the word I will use in this book to express the qualities we want to develop in our children. It should be our goal in rearing children to bring them into God's righteousness.

> Romans 14:17 says: *The kingdom of God is .... righteousness and peace and joy in the Holy Spirit.* It is also order, respect, and the absence of rebellion.

THE DEVELOPMENT OF RIGHTEOUS ORDER

God revealed His righteousness and the importance of order in creation. He began creation by bringing order out of chaos, formlessness (Gen. 1:2). The work of God in creation was to establish that order, and during each day of creation, He was bringing life out of formlessness. Order is necessary to sustain life.

God first separated light from darkness so light could cause things to grow, sustaining life. He separated the waters above and below. The dry land appeared, and He called it earth, and the waters He called seas. He placed seed in the ground and vegetation grew. Plants yielded seeds and trees bore fruit with seeds in them. Then He separated day from night which formed the days, years, seasons; the sun for the day, and the moon to govern the night. He also placed the stars in their places. Next He created living creatures for the waters, birds for the earth and heavens and all the creatures that move, and commanded them all to be fruitful and multiply. Every living thing had its order.

On the sixth day, God created cattle, creeping things on the ground, and then man and woman. In Genesis 1:26 God said, *Let Us make man in Our image, according to Our likeness.* They were to rule over every living thing that moves over the earth. On the seventh day, He established rest and blessed the seventh day and sanctified it, and the order was complete.

Thus, God established an order for all living things. He introduced the concept of seed, and allowed man to rule over all He had created. The seed grows because it is nurtured with light, earth, and water. Man also bears seed, and that seed also needs nurturing. In God's order, there is a father and a mother to nurture the seed that becomes a child. Both are extremely important to the development of a normal human being. God desires a righteous seed.

GOD'S ORDER IN MAN'S SOCIETY

We next see God's order of righteousness in the Ten Commandments (Ex. 20). When He gave the commandments to Moses, He established an order which was to form the foundation for a righteous nation, and every other society. The commandments were to be the moral basis for communal life, bringing necessary order and direction for living.

These commandments were not a passing whim, which God later winked at and laid aside. They were the basic foundation for righteousness without which man cannot attain holiness. These commandments were so important to God that He wrote them with His own hand in stone for Moses. Order is necessary for the life of a society. Notice the following:

In the fifth commandment, we are told that children are to honor their parents, thus establishing God's peace and honor in the home.

In the sixth commandment, we are told not to murder, thus establishing God's order for life in society.

In the seventh commandment, we are told not to commit adultery, thus establishing the covenant relationship of marriage within God's order. The health and stability of the home is dependent upon this order.

In the eighth commandment, we are told not to steal, thus establishing God's order and security in our personal lives.

In the ninth commandment, we are told not to bear false witness against our neighbor, thus establishing justice, peace, and security in God's righteous order.

In the tenth commandment, we are told not to covet anything that belongs to our neighbor, thus instituting restraint, self control, and contentment, which guards us from exploitation by the world system.

If you are not keeping these commandments, you cannot be holy, and you cannot be pleasing to God. Only a righteous seed lives in God's righteous order.

When God sent His only begotten Son, Jesus Christ, to earth, He sent a living example of righteousness and holiness. We are able to see through His example that it is possible to bring order and godliness into our lives and to live by it *And being found in appearance as a man, He humbled Himself by becoming obedient to the point of death, even death on a cross* (Philippians 2:8).

Obedience was the central key of Christ's life. The righteousness that He demonstrated was brought forth and lived out as He conformed to His Father's will in all things. He was obedient even to the suffering of death on the cross. Through His death, He secured pardon for all men who will receive it and brought righteousness to the sinner. His was the ultimate obedience, Jesus was a righteous seed.

Chapter Two

Order in the Home

In light of the order God has established in creation and in society, it seems only reasonable that He has also established an order for the home. If we follow that order, our homes will prosper. If we do things our way or use our own understanding, we will ultimately fail. We must understand His plan and follow it if our children are to be formed in righteousness.

WHAT IS THAT ORDER FOR THE HOME?

In Genesis 3:16, we see God putting man in charge.

> Ephesians 5:25 says: *Husbands, love your wives, just as Christ also loved the church and gave Himself up for her.*

The man then is to be in charge, ruling out of love.

> Ephesians 5:22 says: *Wives be subject to your own husbands, as to the Lord. For the husband is the head of the wife, as Christ also is the head of the church... As the church is subject to Christ, so also the wives ought to be to their husbands in everything.*

These two things are not cultural preferences but principles of the Kingdom. When they are practiced in godliness and humility, they bring forth a home that operates in order and peace.

> Ephesians 6:1 says: *Children, obey your parents in the Lord, for this is right.*

This Scripture establishes the principle of "hear and obey" as the attitude God intends for the children in the home. It is our mandate from God to bring forth children who have the attitude of the righteous.

WHAT IS THE ATTITUDE OF THE RIGHTEOUS?

In Luke 1:17, an angel told the father of John the Baptist that John would turn the disobedient to the attitude of the righteous, so as to make ready a people prepared for the Lord. What is the attitude of the righteous? Listen to these Scriptures that speak of the attitude of the righteous:

> Exodus 19:5 says: *If you will indeed obey My voice and keep My covenant, then you shall be My own possession (or special treasure) among all the people"*

> Isaiah 1:19 says: *If you consent and obey, you will eat the best of the land.*

> Deuteronomy 6:3-4 says: *O Israel, you should listen and be careful to do it, that it may be well with you.... Hear, O Israel! The LORD is one God.*

> Ezekiel 12:2 says: *You live in the midst of the rebellious house, who have eyes to see but do not see, ears to hear but do not hear; for they are a rebellious house.*

These Old Testament Scriptures reveal the heart of the righteous. Their attitude is "to hear and obey." The refusal to hear is part of disobedience and rebellion.

> Jeremiah 11:4b says: *Listen to My voice and do accord-*

ing to all which I command you; so you shall be My people, and I will be your God.

God solemnly warned Israel, "Listen to My voice." Then in Jeremiah 11:14b, He says that because they refuse to listen, *I will not hear them in the time that they cry unto me in their trouble.*

Read Jeremiah 11: 1-17 and you will see that God always dealt with Israel in this way. The one thing He required in keeping His covenant was that they "hear and obey." Today, He has the same attitude toward those who refuse to hear and obey. The Bible is filled with His words on this subject.

"Hearing and obeying" is the attitude of the righteous. We need to work toward creating the spirit of "hear and obey" in our children so righteousness and godliness can be formed in them and they can reap the blessings of God.

When we teach our children to hear and obey, we are discipling them for eternity. This is essential preparation for them to learn to live for (and later with) God; that is, to hear His instructions, to obey Him without rebellion, and to do it with purpose and a good attitude.

Realizing this should impress upon us the importance of discipline in the lives of our children. If they never learn to hear and obey their earthly parents, how can they learn to hear and obey God?

Children live what they learn, and they learn what they live. If they refuse to learn obedience, the negative spirit or sin nature they were born with will take over and set them up for a lifetime of disobedience. You must start when they are very young. And you must be quietly firm, loving and consistent in your efforts. Be diligent in developing an attitude of "hearing and

PRESERVING A RIGHTEOUS SEED

obeying" in your children so righteousness and godliness can be formed in them. If they are old enough to understand what you say in other areas, you can teach them to "hear and obey." A home where the children have learned this is a home at peace. God is waiting for a righteous seed! Seed that will hear and obey His voice.

Chapter Three

The Importance of Father/I

It is almost incomprehensible that we can go to God, the Creator of the universe for help. We can do this because He is a father with a father's heart and a father's authority. He is approachable and desires that we know Him. One of the most wonderful revelations of the Bible is that God is our Father.

If we miss the fact that God is a father, we can easily buy into many of the modern ideas of who God is and fail to understand God's purposes entirely. The reason God is a father is that He chooses to be a father. He could have lived for Himself and avoided the pain of loving rebellious children. But our God had a desire for children, and He acted on that desire.

God is the prototype or original pattern from which copies (in this case fathers) are made. In other words, He gave us an example of fatherhood by showing us His father's heart and His fatherly authority. He passed on to man the ability to love as a father and extended His authority to the man in the home so that a righteous seed could be established in the earth.

The human father is to be the image of the father in heaven, and he is to work with and disciple his children in the same way God does. A father meets his children's physical needs and provides spiritual guidance so they can be molded into a righteous seed that fills the earth for God's glory.

This becomes the challenge for every man who chooses to become a father, even those who become fathers negligently. Will you cooperate with God and do your part in His plan? Will you dedicate your life to bring forth a righteous seed for the Lord? God has a plan, and that plan is for children to have a father who imitates Him.

Almost any man can be a father, but to be a godly father is difficult. In order to produce the desired results, his focus must be in his home. He must forsake all others and love his wife. He must guard against sexual and moral impurity.

If children experience the wise and protective love and guidance of a godly human father's heart, many of the problems they face today will be defused and dissipated. A godly father can provide for his children a clear picture of who God is and who they are supposed to be.

Unfortunately, many fathers have made a god of their own invention rather than modeling themselves after the father heart of God. They imagine that they can raise godly children while living as they want and ignoring God's command to be like Him.

A FATHER'S HEART

It takes a father's heart and a father's authority to form the soul of a child in righteousness.

The image we have of God as Father is created in large part by our relationship with our earthly father. If we rear our children under the spirit of the world rather than the spirit of God, we are likely to push success, production, recognition, and position. Acceptance in our performance-oriented society is always conditional. The kingdom of this world is a kingdom of rejection.

The kingdom of God, however, is a kingdom of unfailing love. It does not fail us because we fail or fall short. God is not vindictive toward our weaknesses, but impartial. He is not swayed by our looks or personality. In fact, He numbers the hairs of our heads, which should indicate to us how intimately He knows us and cares about our lives. His heart toward us is a model for all fathers. Let's take a closer look.

First, we must understand that God's heart is predisposed to love His children (the Bible calls them "seed"). His desire is always turned toward them. Reproducing, developing and perfecting them is the business of His kingdom.

Second, God's heart is a heart of love, loyalty, faithfulness, goodness, mercy, and kindness toward those He has formed in His own image. He communicates with them, makes Himself accessible to them, and pours out His compassion on them. His desire is that we, His children, know Him and feel that we can approach Him. Deuteronomy 32:4 says that He is a God of faithfulness and without injustice.

He will never desert His children. He is a God of protection, provision, warmth, tenderness, gentleness, loving kindness, and justice. He is slow to anger, a forgiving father who delights in being merciful and wants to be intimately involved with each detail of our lives. He is neither stingy, possessive, nor materialistic.

This Scripture reveals another side of God:

> Romans 11:22 says: *Behold then the kindness and severity of God; to those who fell, severity, but to you, God's kindness, if you continue in His kindness; otherwise, you also will be cut off.*

God is a God of kindness, but He can be very severe as well, even to the point of cutting people off from His kindness. This is the attitude that God must take in order to preserve His righteousness.

Rearing children is serious business. Fathers, study the heart of God and do your best to walk like Him in character and disposition. Remember that the aim of godly childrearing is to reproduce His character, His emotions, His attributes in our children. Do so, and your influence will last your child for a lifetime.

THE AUTHORITY OF GOD

God's authority is not harsh and vindictive, but to the contrary He is unspeakably gentle and long suffering. God sits on a throne, which is His position of authority. He sits there, not because He has a great big ego that says, "Look at me! I am great!" Rather, He sits there because He is a father and He is faithful to the creatures He has created. He sits there to see that His righteousness and justice are maintained through His eternal vigilance.

God's order of righteousness for man is not programmed into man. We are not like the animals who live and perform as they are programmed to do. The heart and desire of God is that man bear His image because he chooses to do so. More than that, it is God's desire that man choose to be obedient and separate himself from anything that would lead him away from God's righteousness.

God's authority over us and His heart of love causes us to conform to His righteousness. We become like Him as we separate ourselves to Him in obedience and choose His will first over our own.

God is a disciplinarian. The Bible says that the person whom the Lord loves, He disciplines.

Hebrews 12:4-11 says: *You have not yet resisted to the point of shedding blood in your striving against sin; and you have forgotten the exhortation which is addressed to you as sons, 'My son, do not regard lightly the discipline of the Lord, nor faint when you are reproved by Him; for those whom the Lord loves He disciplines, and He scourges every son whom He receives.'*

He disciplines us for our good that we may share His holiness. God's idea of rearing children is to show His love for them by chastising them when needed. If we do not discipline our children when they need it, we are not operating in the kind of righteous love our Father God has for us.

I Timothy 4:7 says: *Discipline yourself for the purpose of godliness.*

This is the purpose of discipline, to form godliness. For discipline to be effective, there has to be authority behind it and the purpose of authority is to establish and maintain order. As He brings us into order, He ultimately brings us into the freedom and righteousness of God's kingdom.

The opposite of authority is lawlessness. In lawlessness the flesh rules over us. We become subject to lust and sin. The characteristics of a home established in lawlessness are: disorder, conflict, isolation, co-dependence, self-pride, unresolved complaints and issues, and an extreme amount of self-centeredness.

Authority and discipline are so terribly important in the formation of our homes. They will not happen on their own; they must be intentionally instituted. Listen to this Scripture:

Isaiah 32:17 says: *The work of righteousness will be*

peace and the service of righteousness, quietness and confidence forever."

What a tremendous verse for the home. Our children need peace, quietness, and confidence. These qualities can only be acquired by the establishment of righteousness, which comes through order and discipline.

How children respond to God's authority is often influenced by their experience with human authority. Children unconsciously tend to attach the feelings and impressions of their own earthly fathers to their concept of the heavenly Father.

It is God's will for children to see His love revealed through parental tenderness, mercy, and discipline. As a parent, we begin to understand God's heart toward us as His children. There are no perfect parents as there are no perfect children. You will feel like a failure if you depend upon yourself to be a perfect parent. Only God fills that billing. Let God work in your family without interference.

Humanism, the religion of this present age, denies authority and focuses on self. Self-fulfillment realized by "my happiness," "my potential," "my rights" makes Me the center of everything. We make a god of ourselves by putting our own interests before anything or anyone else in our lives. Unless we want our children to grow up lawless and self-centered, we must learn both to establish order and train our children in selflessness.

WHAT ABOUT MOTHERS?

In my emphasis on the father, we must realize his position does not make the woman inferior or unimportant; rather, it establishes headship under which the mother shares his authority. Authority in the home should come through both parents. Rearing children requires the effort of both father and mother.

The mother's part then is to participate in forming a righteous seed for God by submitting to the authority of her husband. This means that when it is her place to do so, she must operate in the same authority her husband operates in. Though God has instituted a formula of shared authority, He has given the responsibility of headship to the father.

A woman establishes or destroys the father's authority over her children by submitting or not submitting to her husband. If she does not respect and joyfully uphold her husband, she runs the risk of rearing children who reject all forms of authority in their lives.

A woman gives more than physical life to her offspring. She gives a core of wholeness to them as she establishes godly respect and honor toward the father in the home. As she submits to her husband, she establishes his authority over her children and her household. A man who does not receive respect in his own home and is emasculated, generally is unable to give love. And there is another danger-if the mother establishes authority apart from her husband, a confusion about sexual identity could result in her children.

Submission on the part of the mother should be given rather than forced. However, a wise woman will consistently choose to submit. It takes conviction on her part that submission is right, and determination to release control to her husband, especially since an attitude of submission conflicts so forcefully with our present culture. It takes a strong woman to take a stand in the midst of an avalanche of culture flowing in the opposite direction.

Submission is not really a cultural issue but spiritual in nature.

It will work anywhere in any culture. By following God's order and working at it, godly mothers can transform their homes. It is a privilege to follow a godly husband.

AUTHORITY WORKS THROUGH LOVE

Authority works through love, and there must be a balance between love and authority. Love wrongly used and authority without love can become harsh and critical, even tyrannical. In other words, rules without relationship bring rebellion.

The love we operate in must be a mature love rather than sentimentality. It must see into the future and understand the end result of the actions we take or fail to take. When we operate in what we believe to be love, but fail to uphold any authority, we rear children who are self-centered and self-willed.

I often hear parents say, "I love my child too much to abuse them by spanking them." But, is this mature, godly love? We must love our children enough to correct them in a Biblical way and make them pleasing in God's eyes. It is His eyes we must please, not our own hearts. He does not just look beyond our sins because He loves us, but He says, "Change. Be like Me. Bring your children into My order."

MOTHERS ESTABLISH THE ATMOSPHERE OF THE HOME

With joy and enthusiasm plus submission to the authority over her, a mother can establish an atmosphere that is healthy and conducive to rearing righteous children.

Mothers usually have a great capacity for intimacy and nurturing, both physically and spiritually. Fathers have more of a spirit of assertiveness and strength. A child needs both. If you as a wife deliberately try to stifle the strength your husband can provide, you may ultimately destroy your marriage and cause confusion in your children.

Remember Peter's statement in I Peter 3:4, which says *The imperishable quality of a gentle and quiet spirit is precious in the sight of God.* This gentleness and quietness does not mean weakness. It means power under control and it forms the basis for godly character in your children. Many mothers who stay home develop an angry attitude toward their children because they have not established their authority. Children reared under this angry attitude pass on the anger to their own children.

A father who will not take authority, nor acknowledge the mother's position and defend her in her position of authority, destroys the authority in the home as surely as a wife who refuses to submit.

A FINAL WORD TO FATHERS

Proverbs 17:6 says: *The glory of sons is their fathers.*

Many of you fathers are giving your children a bad impression of what the Father in heaven is like. You stand in an important position and your responsibilities are awesome. It is prudent to remember that your position as the authority in your children's lives has little to do with you and everything to do with establishing the righteous seed of God.

I would urge you to get serious about your job and ask for God's help daily. No matter what you may have been taught, the Bible does not say that the wife bears the major responsibility for rearing the children. It is you who must answer to God. What an awesome privilege to have the lineage of God's righteous seed coming through you.

PRESERVING A RIGHTEOUS SEED

A FINAL WORD TO MOTHERS

Beware of feminism. This philosophy has some good points, but not many. Over all, it may be one of the most destructive forces in the world today. Do not be deceived. In the light of God's eternal plan, feminism does not have eternal value but godly motherhood does.

If you realize how important your place is in the home, you will not be anxious to leave home to work unless you absolutely have to. Finally, remember Psalms 68: 12, *She who remains at home will divide the spoil.* I believe this is an eternal concept. You will share equally with your husband in the eternal reward of rearing righteous seed if you follow God's plan.

I am well aware of the difficulties involved in this way of thinking. Our enemy, the devil, will use any means available to him to destroy your home. By doing this, he hopes to destroy any hope of a righteous seed. You must be awake and aggressively resist the destroyer of our homes.

Many homes have already been disrupted by divorce or death leaving a mother to fight on alone. In this case, circumstances may force her to take the authority alone. It is a heavy burden, but millions of women are struggling heroically to shoulder the load and bring their children through.

If you find yourself in this place, lean on the Lord and submit yourself to His authority. Nothing will be impossible to you when you put your trust in God.

A CHECKLIST FOR FATHERS

As a father, you should be able to say, "Be like me." Noah's sons followed him into the ark. Are your children following you into the ark of safety? You cannot force them in; they must follow you. Remember, it is never too late to be a godly father. Consider the following checklist to help you develop a heart like God's toward your children:

1. *Love their mother more.* Let your children see unity between you and their mother.
2. *Touch your children more.* Even grown children need hugs and assurances of your love.
3. *Listen to them more.* Sit and relax and focus on them. Children do not just grow, they are formed.
4. *Look for more opportunities to give your children a sense of belonging.*
5. *Give more personal and sincere appreciation, not just praise for success.*
6. *Laugh a lot more.* You bring sunshine or the lack of it into the home. Laughter is a blessing. Use it to make your home a happier place.
7. *Talk more about the positive power of Christ to change people's lives.* Teach them the commandments of the Lord.
8. *Give them your blessings.* There is comfort in blessing.
9. *Pray for them and call their names in prayer.*
10. *Establish strong boundaries.* Strong boundaries set children free.
11. *Lead your children.* To teach without training is to fail at your task.
12. *Uphold the position of their mother by defending them.*

The father heart of God was manifested when He sent His only begotten Son, Jesus, to live a flawless life and give Himself as a sacrifice for our sins. Jesus accepted the will of His father and acted in obedience, even to death on a cross. Because of the righteousness and order in the Godhead, we have a clear picture of what a father should be.

PRESERVING A RIGHTEOUS SEED

Chapter Four

Satan Has a Plan for Your Child

You have probably heard it said that "God has a wonderful plan for your life." But, did you know that the devil also has a plan for your life and the lives of your children as well?

As Christian parents, we must always remember that Satan's intent is to destroy our children and thus, destroy the righteous seed of God. In many cases, we will be asked to fight to the death for the lives and souls of our children. That will never change while we are here on earth.

The age of God's grace is drawing to a close, and the devil knows that his time is short. He is merciless and violent, and we must constantly be aware that he will fight us with every foul trick and scheme that he can muster. Are you prepared to battle him?

You can win over Satan's tactics. It just takes a little knowledge, a little faith, and the will to stand for those you love so much.

> Genesis 4:7 says: *If you do well, will not your countenance be lifted up? And if you do not do well, sin is crouching at the door; and its desire is for you, but you must master it.* We can master and overcome the evil plan Satan has for us and our children.
>
> I Corinthians 16:13-4 says: *Be on the alert, stand firm in the faith, act like men, be strong. Let all that you do be done in love.*

SATAN HAS MANY STRATEGIES

Our genes pass on to our children the sins of our fathers. This means that our children are sometimes born with what amounts to inherited curses. I would encourage you to read Exodus 20:5, 34:7; Leviticus 26:39; Numbers 14:18, 33; Deuteronomy 5:9; Job 21:19; Psalm 37:28; Proverbs 14:11; Isaiah 14:20,21; Jeremiah 32:18; Lamentations 5:7.

These curses can include a spirit of anger, sexual perverseness, an inordinate sexual desire, and rejection. There can also be a transmission caused by other circumstances before birth.

Some babies are born with a predisposition that life is not good. This is a mysterious thing and it is very real. There is communication in the womb. The baby does not think with words, but it is sensitive to feelings, attitudes, and both negative and positive physical stimuli such as noise or music.

Although I cannot verify the authenticity of this story, I once read that an experiment was undertaken by scientists to determine the effect of cigarette smoke on an unborn baby. To their surprise, they discovered that the baby squirmed every time the mother thought about getting a cigarette. Somehow the baby seemed to know what was coming.

> Psalm 139:13,14 says: *For Thou didst form my inward parts; Thou didst weave me in my mother's womb. I will give thanks to Thee, for I am feaifully and wondeifully made.*

Another strategy of Satan is to inflict so much pain and hurt into a child's life that he or she cannot recover. Such an individual may remain wounded for life and never pose a threat to the kingdom of darkness.

One devastating area of hurt and disaster is divorce. The world tries to make us believe children are not always hurt by divorce. This simply is not true. In 45 years of ministry (the last 28 in counseling and deliverance), my husband can tell you that it is rare indeed for a child not to be wounded by the divorce or death of a parent. Some never recover.

If Satan cannot destroy the child through his or her parents, he will attack the child through his or her self image. Few of us totally escape this ploy, and the damage can begin even in the womb. Unwanted babies sense they are not wanted even though they are not aborted.

A child's self image can also be destroyed by the words, actions, and attitudes of other people, often their parents or their peers. One advantage of home-schooling is the escape of a lot of the negative peer pressure.

A third strategy of Satan is to steal our children's hearts through the lust of sin in the world. Not only does this destroy their souls, but it steals the very years of their lives and may destroy you and your faith and witness in the process. In fact, a whole family can be negatively affected by the works of Satan in the life of a child.

Television is a culprit here because it facilitates the hero worship of movie stars and their lifestyles, which can quickly lead the young astray. For the most part, the world has lost its true heroes to the glitter, glitz, and immorality of Hollywood and the TV industry. In order to safeguard your children, you must be willing to examine what you watch on television. Children are likely to put more stock in what you do than what you say.

A good rule is not to allow anything to enter your home that you would not want your children to love. This includes rock music, some television, and computer games that are less than wholesome.

PRESERVING A RIGHTEOUS SEED

Satan may also use circumstances to attack your children. Every circle of people your children are exposed to has an impact on them: grandparents, aunts, uncles, siblings, the church soccer team, football team. Where you live also has an effect on the lives of your children. That influence can be good and righteous or lewd and perverted. Where there is unrighteousness there is the potential for every evil work.

The personality of the parent has a great impact on the lives of the children. It is passed on to them as a heritage. Some areas that are passed on are easy to detect such as anger, fear, unhappiness, and overindulgence.

If you are sullen and withdrawn, your children may think your unhappiness is somehow their fault. This is often true when children must deal with the divorce of their parents.

If you find yourself in this situation, pull yourself together and smile into their eyes, even if you do not feel like it. Put on a happy spirit! Do not take out your own unhappiness on your children, or anyone else for that matter. If you do not have a happy spirit, develop one!

You can, you know. You don't have to stay with the introverted, unhappy spirit you were born with or have developed because of unhappy circumstances in your life. Thwart the devil's strategy by changing your personality. Develop! Mature! Practice being happy, smiling into your child's eyes and your husband's as well. It will change your life and the life in your home.

In the end, the ministry of Jesus is our "court of last resort." When we have done what we can do, there is Jesus. He can be depended upon to help us defeat the plan of Satan to destroy our children. If you and your mate will pray regularly together, covering your children, you will not have to resort to an emergency measure.

Chapter Five

"Stuff" on the Hard Drive (p k)

A little girl says to her friend, "I'm not having any kids! I hear they take nine months to download." Download is a computer term meaning to transfer data from one storage device or system to another. The downloading or gestation and birth of a baby is only the beginning of the making of a human being. It takes much more than nine months to develop a righteous being fit for the house of God in eternity.

My daughter, who works with computers, says that after you download, you have a program on a new disk, but some refining is required to make it fit its new environment. In other words, there is "stuff" on the hard drive with which we have to deal.

Years ago, there was a common saying which said, "Children are blank pages for which we are totally responsible." It only took one child to make me aware that I was dealing with "stuff," the origins of which I could not begin to identify. This "stuff" was unlike me in any way, and it certainly bore no resemblance to my calm, patient husband.

My first child was born in constant motion with a mind of his own. I barely got him home from the hospital before we began to have difficulty. His constant restlessness made me so nervous that I had no breast milk. That made him angry and he would stiffen and scream until someone provided what he needed to satisfy his hunger. It was a constant cycle.

PRESERVING A RIGHTEOUS SEED

As much as I failed to see any connection to our own personalities, I knew that our child's hard drive was programmed with "stuff" inherited genes from his parents. All children inherit a predisposition toward certain "stuff" and much of that "stuff" is negative. This can manifest in unnatural anger, sexual perversions and rebellion at an early age. Some characteristics are well established before the end of the first year of life.

The good news is we do not have to live with the bondage of sin handed down to us generationally through the bondage of our parents. Freedom is available for us in Jesus Christ. We must be washed by His blood and have our sins forgiven.

Salvation takes care of many of these types of bondage, but if you are still tormented and have not worked through to freedom from the sins of your youth and your own inherited sins, get before God until you are free.

If you do not seem to be able to break free on your own, find a church with a deliverance ministry that can help you. There is a tremendous need for the help of the deliverance ministry in our churches today.

We cannot be directly blamed for the problems we have inherited. But our responses are often sinful, and these still have to be dealt with. The fact is that we are responsible and daily accountable for how we handle anger, sexual perversion and rebellion. We have to see these things as sin and not just the normal response of mankind.

Confess these things as sins and gain freedom. When we have confessed and received forgiveness, then we are free ourselves and we can minister "life" to our children.

Pray for your unborn children, releasing them from inherited sins. Remember, the prayers of the righteous bring great results.

Chapter Six

Dealing With Rebellion

Rebellion is a serious sin. Unfortunately, most parents today do not realize how God looks at this problem.

> I Samuel 15:23 says: *For rebellion is as the sin of witchcraft(divination) and insubordination(stubbornness: unreasonable, obstinate, unyielding, inflexible) is as iniquity and idolatry.*

We do not think of our precious children and their disobedience as the same rebellion referred to in this Scripture. In reality, a rebellious, headstrong child is beginning a life of disobedience. In the Scripture above, Saul was rejected as King of Israel because of a rebellious spirit. His rebellion cost him the kingdom. Israel itself was a rebellious and stiff-necked people, and it cost them the Promised Land. Let's see what more the Scriptures have to say about rebellion:

> Psalm 78:8 says: *A stubborn and rebellious generation, a generation that did not prepare its heart, and whose spirit was not faithful to God.* Read Psalm. 78:1-8 as well.

> Proverbs 17: 11: *A rebellious man seeks only evil.*

> In Isaiah 1: 13, God says, *I cannot endure iniquity.*

These are only a few Scriptures that tell us how God looks at rebellion. We must do our part to keep our children from falling into this trap of Satan. Rebellion sometimes starts at a young age. I have seen very small children who are full of rage and disobedience (rebellion).

HOW DO WE DEAL WITH THE REALITY OF A REBELLIOUS CHILD?

Rebellion is one of the most difficult problems you will have to deal with as a parent. Here are some pointers:

1. Start young! It is shocking how early problems with rebellion start to develop in our children. Don't allow that spirit to go unchecked! When you see it developing, use all your creativity and prayer power to build into your children a spirit of submission. Submission is not an *act* (or acts), but an *attitude!*

2. Teach your children not to fall prey to the victim mentality. God is compassionate, but He really will not bless this way of thinking. Ultimately, we are responsible for our sinful responses in life, even when they seem to be justified. Too many children grow up thinking someone else is to blame for the way their lives are turning out. As parents, our responsibility is to lead and guide our children, but ultimately we are not responsible for the choices they make and the subsequent consequences of those choices.

Remember that everyone who comes in contact with your children will have some kind of effect on their lives. Sometimes that influence is positive and sometimes it is negative. We do not have a great deal of control over this, except through prayer! A father and mother, praying in unity is a great force for righteousness in their children's lives.

3. Release your children completely to God and thank Him for them just as they are. God wants to bring glory out of every situation, and He can when our unbelief doesn't hinder Him. Releasing our children does not mean accepting their sin. It means accepting their person and knowing God can work in them as we release them to Him. This is faith in action-faith that works, faith without which we cannot please God.

You will often find this hard to do. We desperately want to "fix" things for our children, save our own reputations, or save ourselves from the pain and sorrow their actions bring. But if we can release them to God and show them love and not rejection, we will see what God can do.

4. *Surrender all your expectations, disappointments, and dreams for your children to the Lord.* Many parents have high expectations for their children. My sister-in-law (a teacher) says she has seen many small children who are afraid to try in school for fear of failing. We must see our children as unique human beings, not extensions of ourselves! We cannot live our lives through them.

As Christians, we can experience extreme disappointment when our children turn their backs on their faith. It is easy to become bitter and antagonistic toward them when this happens. However, our attitude can keep God from helping them.

Sometimes I tell people to take all this hurt, put it in their hands, hold their hands up to God and give it all to Him. He is the only one Who can give peace. He is the only one Who can bring our children through to their God-given potential. They may not be meeting our expectations and dreams, but God can fulfill His will in their lives if we let Him. As parents, it is important for us to allow Him to guide our children and work in them without blocking Him with our anger, bitterness, and sorrow.

PRESERVING A RIGHTEOUS SEED

Enter into praise and thanksgiving that God will intervene to work His will in the life of your child. This calls for strong faith that God is in truth concerned with the perfecting of your child. Faith works when it is according to the will of God!

5. *Operate in forgiveness.*

> Mark 11:25 says: *And whenever you stand praying, forgive, if you have anything against anyone; so that your Father also who is in heaven may forgive you your transgressions.* Verse 26 says, *But if you do not forgive, neither will your Father who is in heaven forgive your transgressions.*

It's not easy to forgive children who have rejected your standards, your love, and sometimes your very person. At times they may have humiliated you, possibly even hurt your ministry. It is easy to develop a critical attitude, hurt feelings, and a spirit of judgment against them.

God does not work in the situation when we do not deal with and correct our own sins. So be quick to deal with your feelings and forgive. Release your pain, your rights, your expectations and love that child, not just in words but in deeds.

6. *Order your conversation right.*

> Job 42:7 says: *You have not spoken of Me what is right.*

Under the pressure of a rebellious child, it is easy to feel that God has forsaken you and give place to resentment. You know God could do something to right the situation and work a miracle, but you don't see anything good happening. When a rescue doesn't happen, we feel God doesn't answer prayer or doesn't love us. Sometimes we may buckle under the guilt and shame of all our sins and believe that God will just let us endure these problems. We need holiness in our lives, so we can stand before God with confidence.

Many people are disappointed when they realize they are not as successful as they had hoped or planned to be in their roles as parents. As a result, they sometimes become bitter against God. This is a dangerous attitude. If you find yourself feeling this way, grab hold of faith and confess the character of God. He is good, full of mercy, long-suffering, and He loves His children. He will work on your behalf; He will answer your prayers. But you must please Him with your faith and speak it to Him.

7. *Don't provoke your children.*

> Ephesians 6:4 warns us, *Do not provoke your children to anger.*

Be kind, be just, be understanding, be helpful, and most of all be mature. A child whose emotions are out of control cannot be helped by a parent who is operating in the same emotional spirit.

Parents should also avoid treating their children like they are just one more of their problems. Give them undivided attention. Look them in the eyes when you talk to them. Give them worth by showing them they are important. Don't return insult for insult. Control yourself, especially your tongue!

Of course there is another side to this. Children must learn their place and learn to give respect. Patiently teach them not to monopolize conversations, nor try to outtalk grow ups. Ironically, if you have to scream at them to get your message across, they will not hear you. Rather set a godly example. Actions always speak louder than words.

PRESERVING A RIGHTEOUS SEED

8. *Count it all joy!*

I am sure some of you have already decided I have lost my mind. But let me tell you, you will not defeat demons or demonic activity with a spirit of depression-one of the natural responses to an out-of-control child. I love to watch children laugh, don't you? God, being a father, wants to see your joy.

> Psalm 149:5,6 says: *Let the godly ones exult in glory; let them sing for joy on their beds. Let the high praises of God be in their mouth, and a two-edged sword in their hand.* This Scripture does not say "if everything is going well with them," or "if they are free from problems."

When life gets out of hand, sing for joy. God is about to show Himself strong. Don't wait for the solution to come before you let the high praises of God come from your mouth. When you are in the midst of the problem, it is the time to show your trust in God by declaring it.

How long will we mourn the trauma of our wayward children as if there is no hope? When we live as if we have no loving Father in heaven who cares for us, it is a poor testimony to those who do not yet know Him. Be finished with sorrow, remorse, and self-pity! God expected to help you when He gave you that child. Show your faith in Him by responding to adversity with joy. Expect a miracle! Rejoice! You are about to see the greatness of God move on your behalf.

9. *Fast and pray.*

The disciples came to Jesus privately regarding a man's son who was a lunatic. Jesus rebuked the demon, it came out of him, and the boy was cured. Later, the disciples asked Jesus why they could not cast the demon out.

Matthew 17: 19-21 says: *And He said to them, 'Because of the littleness of your faith; for truly I say to you, if you have faith as a mustard seed, you shall say to this mountain, 'Move from here to there,' and it shall move; and nothing shall be impossible to you. But this kind does not go out except by prayer and fasting.*

Fasting and prayer bring deliverance and free us from the bondage of the devil.

10. *Expect deliverance from a rebellious spirit.*

Follow these steps, and you will see your children delivered from the grip of Satan's powers. If you know prayer warriors, enlist them in the battle; and if possible, seek the aid of someone who has a proven anointing in deliverance.

11. *Disciple the child.*

When a child makes a move back to sanity and God, do not stop your intercession. Satan has had a stronghold in your child's life and it is not his nature to give up easily. You must stand, and having done all to stand, you must continue to stand steadfast and resolute.

The devil has no right to the seed of the righteous. This is a battle, and if you don't want to leave the battlefield bloody and defeated, you must hold your position and fight. It is a winnable war with God's help. Begin to teach your children again, bringing control into their lives through training in obedience.

12. *Keep your life free from sin.*

> Job 13:23 says: *Make known to me my rebellion and my sin.*

PRESERVING A RIGHTEOUS SEED

We as parents often do not recognize our own rebellion or sin. It is important when we stand before God on behalf of our children that our lives are free of sin. Let the Word of God, the blood of Jesus Christ, and the work of the Holy Spirit cleanse you and make you whole! Ask God to show you in truth where you stand with Him. Our lives should be a purifying agent on earth.

Chapter Seven

Kids Are Like Race Horses

I woke up one morning thinking, "Training a child is like training a race horse." I recognized that God was speaking to me, so I called my oldest son, Victor, who has been involved in raising Russian Arabian horses, and asked him what he could tell me about training a race horse.

To begin with, a horse is put through certain paces over and over until it performs perfectly and automatically. It is given no grass and no water while it goes through these paces. The routine eventually becomes second nature to the horse. He becomes a winner through repetitive discipline.

Just getting around the track is not enough. The horse has to have endurance and a strong spirit to go the distance. The trainer must be careful to build the horse's endurance without breaking its spirit. If the spirit of the horse is broken, it will not make a good racer. In fact, it will not even be good for riding.

The Romans brought their horses from the Greek mountains. These horses were very spirited and strong. "Praus" is the Greek word for "meek," and it means strength under control. It also means tractable, manageable, and submissive. A good race horse should be meek (gentle, tractable, manageable, submissive) with a very strong spirit, which has been brought under control-strength working well under subjection and under discipline.

Meekness is also the goal for our children. Children are running the race of life. We must train and discipline them, bringing them into God's order and righteousness until they are capable of winning this race. This is the principle work of the parent-more important than sports, piano lessons, computer expertise, karate lessons or any worldly pursuit no matter how good, because training our children in righteousness has eternal results.

We try to prepare them to live in this world, but sometimes we fail to prepare them for the world to come. Some day your children must meet God. Will they be winners in the greatest race of all?

There is another similarity between horses and children. Horses have a "pecking order" much the same as chickens. In a group, every horse has a place. If he tries to move out of that place, he is quickly forced back by the other horses, usually the top horse.

A pecking order establishes a child's position in a group. His or her self-concept is acquired by comparison with other kids. Kids will align themselves and become friends with someone they don't even like in order to move up in the pecking order. Even becoming friends with the school bully or a group of hoodlums makes them feel like "somebody" in the eyes of their peers. This can be especially dangerous for a child who does not have a positive home situation.

My son Victor told about an exceptionally bad bully in a Christian grade school he attended. Even though the young boy was cruel and violent, most of the kids wanted to be his friend-probably out of fear for their own safety.

Victor resisted that tactic so the kid tormented him for some time, threatening to beat him up. One day, Victor came to the head of the stairs to go home and the bully and his friends were at the bottom waiting. Victor said he felt like a trapped animal unaccustomed to fighting, and he suddenly went "berserk!" On that day, he faced a vicious school bully, came out a winner, and gained the admiration of the other students.

However, something else happened that day. Victor developed a desire to fight. He began to hate people and to react in anger to any situation. Fortunately, this problem has passed, but his father and I never knew the source of his problems, just that our son was terribly unhappy. When God really got hold of him, the dark thoughts left, and he began to love people. Today he is a good pastor because he loves his people and defends them even from criticism. God took his weakness, his hatred of people, and made it one of his greatest strengths.

I asked Victor why he was so unhappy in his teens. He answered that he wasn't happy with his "self." He believed he did not measure up and felt ashamed of who he was. Most of this came from peer pressure. His "looks" did not please him, and the things that were not said to him or about him were more damaging than anything that was said.

He was attending a private Christian school where some of the children's fathers were doctors and lawyers. His father was only a minister and Bible school teacher. Victor was ashamed of him. Children often make these judgments against their parents. Fortunately, this judgment changed, and today his father is his hero.

There were three things Victor said that made a difference in his turn around.

First of all, he knew that his dad prayed for him daily and never missed his football games. These things gave him an assurance of his father's love.

Second, I kept trying, pleading with him, with a heart to help. This gave him an assurance that I loved him no matter what happened.

Third, Victor attended a Christian high school where the Word of God was read every day and Christian teachers made a difference. Of course, some teachers only saw a kid with problems, but others believed in Victor and began to give him a sense of worth that helped start the healing in him.

As parents, we should not be fooled into thinking that sending our children to Christian schools will guarantee them a better quality of friends. Sometimes the teachers do not even measure up. Even so, any godly influence is helpful and reinforces the teaching from the home. Christian teachers helped Victor break through the depression and negative thought patterns. The Word of God read every day delivered him from dark thoughts and oppression, and with support from home he made it through.

Children are not race horses for they are far more sensitive, complex, extremely challenging, and of infinitely more value. So put your mind, heart and spirit, plus plenty of creativity into training your child. It is a challenge you must accept and take seriously. It is a much higher calling than any career.

There is always hope! Even if the child is demonized, he is never hopeless. With God, nothing is impossible. I remember sitting on the edge of my bed a number of times talking to God and saying, "Father, even You can't change this child." But He did, and He can change yours also!

Parents often have no idea what their kids are like away from home, nor what is happening inside the child's spirit. Sometimes we are angry with God for not helping us more, or for what we believe God is allowing our children to go through. But God uses our experiences, both good and bad. He is a redeeming God, even if the child is wounded.

The will of God in our lives and our children's lives is not automatic. We must do our part to actively wait for God's will to be done. A sixteenth-century church saint said, "The essence of Christianity is to totally abandon yourself to God." This does not mean we are to abandon our responsibilities. But the joining of God's will to man's will places us in a position for God to work through us and in our children. We need to "hear and obey" God so we can teach the principle to our children. As we train our children to "hear and obey" us, we transfer that same spirit of obedience to their relationship to God.

Perhaps something more should be said here concerning bonding and training the will without breaking the spirit of the child. There are several things that will break the spirit of a child:

1. *Unjust treatment.* If one or both parents are too harsh, unloving, judgmental, unconcerned, determined to push the child too hard, or require little or nothing, the child's self worth could be destroyed, leaving him or her defenseless against a hostile world. A child reacts to helplessness by developing a problem with rebellion or becoming passive and building a wall of self-defense for protection. Justice matters!

2. *Faulty training.* A lack of self-control, direction, discipline, and positive, repetitive training, can leave a child with a fragmented spirit and soul. The child may develop a strong spirit, but it will not be a righteous one. And he or she will be unable to run a winning race in life. His parents will receive very little pleasure from his life.

The world tells us that spanking a child is child abuse! God tells us that it is an acceptable means of training a child. How can that be? "Discipline" and "love" go hand in hand. Teaching a child to "hear and obey" is about the most important thing you can do. Even teaching children to love God is unproductive without discipline. They may think they love God but they won't necessarily see a need to honor, respect, and obey Him.

Chapter Eight

Pain Is a Necessary Part of Life

We all avoid pain as much as possible, and why wouldn't we? Our cultural prejudices deny there is any redeeming value whatsoever in pain. We do not "choose" pain, but we still need to recognize its value. Looking back over my own life, I can testify to the fact that pain is often valuable. When our second child and first daughter (Janae) died, God opened the windows of heaven and blessed me with the supernatural comfort of His presence.

I would not have chosen the pain, but strange to say, it probably was the most valuable experience of my life. As a bonus, my little baby daughter is safely "on the other side" without suffering through life here on earth. I truly learned how great God is and how good! Although He inflicts pain, He also gives comfort, faith, healing, and love in return.

> Job 5:17-18 says: *Behold, how happy is the man whom God reproves, so do not despise the discipline of the Almighty. For He inflicts pain, and gives relief; He wounds, and His hands also heal.*

The fact is that when we are broken, when the goodness and safety we expect to be ours is destroyed, when our plans fall apart and our self-sufficiency is not enough, we seem to learn how to love and live better. Pain is one of the building blocks of our lives.

It is important to understand that pain does not always mean that God is displeased with us. God is a loving father, full of wisdom and mercy. He demonstrates His wisdom by showing mercy and bringing correction. Sometimes that involves pain. What is the value of the pain we suffer, what benefits do we gain from it, and what purpose does it accomplish in our lives? Consider this:

1. *Pain ultimately drives us to seek God.* Many of us would never seek, or respond to God if we were not in pain.

2. *Pain brings spiritual and emotional growth and maturity-fast!*

3. *With pain, God breaks through our selfishness and helps break through our walls.*

4. *Pain causes us to reach out to others, a "need" that we have but do not always recognize.*

5. *Pain plows up the fallow, hard ground of our hearts and shows us what is really inside.*

6. *Pain becomes the test of obedience.* We must obey even if it costs us and causes us pain. Will we believe God is somewhere in the pain? Will we believe that even the pain is under His control? Do we believe He has our good in mind even though it appears to be the work of Satan?

> Jeremiah 29: 11 says: *For I know the plans that I have for you' declares the Lord, 'plans for welfare and not for calamity to give you a future and a hope.'*

7. *Pain reveals the attitudes of the heart.* When we are in pain, it is easy for rebellion to creep in. Rebellion is a dangerous response to pain because it brings about more problems than it solves.

8. *When it is allowed, pain becomes the occasion of God's*

mercy. For this to happen, however, we must embrace pain and respond to it correctly.

> James 5:11 says: *You have heard of the endurance of Job and have seen the outcome of the Lord's dealings, that the Lord is full of compassion and is merciful.*

In James 5:10, we see that Job prospered after he prayed for his friends. He came out of his own pain to pray for others. He responded in a positive way to what God allowed, and the Lord increased all that Job had two-fold. It seemed as if Job had lost everything physically and God had turned His back on him. But after his pain and troubles ended, Job lived 140 years and had seven more sons and three more daughters, saw four generations of children and grandchildren. Job died an old man, full of days.

God's blessings fall on those who endure the pain God allows, respond correctly, and stand fast in their faith.

> In Job 42:5,6 Job says, *I have heard of Thee by the hearing of the ear; but now my eye sees Thee.*

After Job repented, he was blessed materially, but more importantly, his spiritual knowledge of God was enlarged and expanded.

Allow pain to drive you into the arms of God. Do not rebel against Him. Most of us do not trust God "first" in our pain. Rather, we blame Him. "Can't He keep it from happening," we ask, "or at least take it away?"

It is also unwise to blame those around us, especially if we believe they are causing or contributing to the pain we are feeling. This type of response is not productive.

An equally inappropriate response is to put the guilt and blame

PRESERVING A RIGHTEOUS SEED

on ourselves. This may seem natural when our children begin to move away from their spiritual upbringing. We tend to ask, "What did we do wrong?" "Where did we fail?" "What can we do to fix the situation?"

If God uses pain, then we must learn to handle it first for ourselves and then in regard to our children. We should pray for godly wisdom concerning how to use the pain our children must endure to mold their lives.

Once we learn to handle pain, we will be able to teach our children how to run to Jesus with their troubles-how to seek Him for healing and learn from their suffering. They will learn to look for what God is saying to them through their pain. Pain will come into each life sooner or later and children who have some understanding of pain will have a much easier time handling life. Children need to know that God is there for them if they do not rebel against Him.

Pain is for purifying our nature, perfecting our obedience, and cleansing our sins. This is the part pain plays in our development and the development of our children. So it is important how we respond to pain and how we administer it. It is used by God to bring us into an attitude of the righteous.

For children to mature properly, we do them a great service to use some pain, if necessary as correction. The Bible stands solidly behind this idea in the Old and New Testaments. Consider these Scriptures:

> Proverbs 13:24 says: *He who spares his rod hates his sons. But he who loves him, disciplines him diligently.*
>
> Proverbs 22: 15 says: *Foolishness is bound up in the heart of a child; the rod of discipline will remove it far from him.*

> Proverbs 23: 13 says: *Do not hold back discipline from the child, although you beat him with the rod, he will not die. You shall beat him with the rod, and deliver his soul from Sheol.* This Scripture is often quoted by God-haters as child abuse. It is often overlooked by multitudes who do not understand God or His ways.
>
> Proverbs 29:15 says: *The rod and reproof gives wisdom, but a child who gets his own way brings shame to his mother.*
>
> Ephesians 6: 1-4 says: *Children, obey your parents in the Lord for this is right. Honor your father and mother (which is the first commandment with a promise), that it may be well with you. Fathers, do not provoke your children to anger; but bring them up in the discipline and instruction of the Lord."*

It is a common thing today to find parents, especially mothers, who believe that inflicting any kind of physical pain is not loving the child. Biblically, not loving your children is allowing them to persist in their self-centered, headstrong, rebellious ways! This only leads your children to years of empty lives and unhappiness as their ways bring them constant frustration, disaster, and pain that they do not have the knowledge or will to change. The world will not be as kind to your child as you see yourself being.

Oh yes, there is abuse in this area and probably always has been. Children have been abused because of the inappropriate anger, rage, frustration, and lack of godliness demonstrated by immature and self-centered adults. It is easy to see why most people who do not have a biblical background would see using pain as an inappropriate way to correct children.

Sometimes parents are reluctant to discipline their children

PRESERVING A RIGHTEOUS SEED

with physical pain because of the anger and rebellion they felt after being spanked as a child. These individuals may have been spanked unjustly or in an inappropriate or overly harsh manner. And sometimes, a parent's reluctance is due to the rebellion in his or her own heart.

Pain for children who refuse to hear and obey is an effective disciplinary tool when it is administered in justice and mercy.

It must also be noted that there are some parents who were whipped quite thoroughly and are glad for it because it changed them in positive ways, which they now recognize and appreciate.

Children should be treated with as much respect as any adult and there should never be a sense of superior power that takes advantage of the weak. Children should not be disciplined for accidents or "hit" simply because the parent feels like hitting something.

I have seen small children who duck every time one of their parents raise a hand because they have grown to expect to be hit. It is always wrong to hit a child out of meanness or because we are so frustrated we just feel like beating on someone who is defenseless and handy.

Children should never be punished in an undisciplined manner. Parents should always be in control of themselves, and the child should understand for what he is being punished. It is easy to take revenge when children push us to the edge. We should not allow negative behavior to continue until we are pushed too far. Discipline should always be a positive act to bring the child into line with righteousness.

It is the nature of evil to inflict pain on the innocent. Children and teenagers are often in pain. As adults, we fail to see why they are in such misery, nor are we very sympathetic to it. Often this pain turns to bitterness. The result is a broken spirit, depression, bitterness, rebellion, drugs, and a myriad of other problems connected to these feelings of hopelessness.

In teens and small children, the pain they receive from their siblings and peers is extremely hurtful, and their self-images can be destroyed or badly hurt. Children can be cruel, and many young people today seem to have little conscience when it comes to the feelings of others.

Parents need to recognize that children, for the most part, do not like to be different. They speak the language of the country where they live. When they change countries, they change languages. They want to look like the children with whom they are friends. In public schools there is great pressure to perform, to look a certain way, to like and conform to certain styles, even to talk a certain way. Christian children are often torn between wanting to fit into the world system they are forced to live in and the desire to please their parents and God.

Those who are taught at home miss a lot of this excessive pressure, and they are not forced to fight for survival in the schools before they are strong enough to cope. They have definite advantages and generally seem to have an easier time with life.

Parents can cause great pain for their children, sometimes without even knowing it. If there is no love or stability in the home, the child's security is destroyed. Parents who fight in front of their children seem to have no concept of the damage they are causing in their children's lives. Even fighting in the bedroom where the noise and anger can be heard through the walls is devastating. No wonder so many young children commit suicide. To them the world is seemingly not a good place to be, and they want "out" whatever the cost.

Parents who divorce also cause extreme pain for children. Our self-centered culture has convinced us that children survive divorce quite well. Most do manage to go on living, and some even overcome. But in spite of all your statistics, my husband and I can tell you after 28 years in counseling and deliverance, that divorce is extremely difficult for all children. Some are hurt so badly they carry that pain with them for the rest of their lives.

My aim is not to put blame or guilt on anyone. I am just stating the results of what happens. When God said, "I hate divorce," I believe He was partly referring to the fall-out of divorce. The children, usually the innocent, are wounded. Either one or both spouses are wounded or nearly destroyed. No wonder God says He hates divorce, and then says at the end of that verse, *"So take heed to your spirit, that you do not deal treacherously."*

Finally, some things I have learned along the way:

1. *Do not wear your pain for your children to see.* When you do this, you are telling them there is no hope. A depressed parent robs the home of joy. It is also an open door for Satan to work.

2. *Accept pain as an opportunity to grow and to bring you closer to Christ.* Trials are meant to make you strong. God brings us into maturity through the things we suffer. Let pain bring you into maturity as a parent. Hebrews 5:8 says that even Jesus learned obedience through the things He suffered.

3. *Learn to truly trust God to answer your prayers for your children with His wisdom and not your own.* You must totally trust Him with their lives.

Every fiber of a mother's being is tuned to bringing life to her children and sustaining that life both physically and spiritually. It is our heart's greatest desire that they learn to love God as we love Him. It is our hope that His comfort will be theirs through life and that they will have an eternal home with our Father who is in heaven. So it is natural, in the flesh, to panic when we begin to see evidence of Satan's work in their lives. With some children, this is evident at a very early age; but whatever the age, panic is not going to help. Faith in God is the answer.

I began to learn to trust with my second child, Nina (Nena) Janae. Born in Brazil, she seemed to always be getting sick. For 5 1/2 months, I struggled to keep her alive only to lose the battle on July 11, 1965. That was my first experience with the pain of loss of life, and I experienced it deep in the heart of Brazil without my family or my husband present.

But Someone was there. God came to me and walked every step of the way with me. What I experienced at that time gave me a fantastic look at a faithful God who allows pain but comforts supernaturally when we reach out to Him. Janae's death brought spiritual gifts into my life that have followed me for 30 years, and I can tell you that when you accept the will of the Father, His blessings will follow you, overtake you, and overwhelm you!

The thing He asks of us is that we choose Him, reach out for Him, and trust Him with our lives and the lives of those we love. He wants us to abandon ourselves and allow Him a free hand in every area. God is fantastic! Try Him! If you see your children beginning to stray from the will of God, start putting your faith to work. God wants to give you a testimony of His faithfulness.

4. *Our greatest suffering comes from watching our children suffer.* Usually we will do all we can to help and some of the

time, this is fine. But do not try to be everything to your children. Let God be God. Let Him work, and do not get in His way by taking all the pain out of their lives. Keep pointing them to the One who has all the answers until they can seek Him for themselves.

5. *God uses our children to perfect righteousness in our lives.* We learn so much from rearing children. That's why I believe so strongly that we are the key to rearing godly children. If we allow God to work in us, we will do a much better job. The best teachers are those who have experienced what they teach.

6. *We must take responsibility for our lives, and our children must take responsibility for their actions and responses to what life hands out.* We cannot choose who is going to hurt us, but we can choose how we respond to that hurt. You can overcome your difficulties, in Jesus' Name, if you want to.

7. *Joy in the home is so important, but being a parent can be tiring, time consuming, aggravating, and demanding.* We must work to keep as much happiness and peace in our homes as possible. My friend with eight children told me how much she enjoyed rearing her children. She couldn't wait for summer to come. She is an energetic, happy, godly woman, and she and her husband have reared great kids with only one child rebelling in her young years.

My husband has often said that the mother sets the atmosphere of the home. I believe that is basically true. Through joy and enthusiasm, we can set an atmosphere that will benefit our children throughout their lives. Besides, that is true godliness! Depression, irritability, nasty responses, and impatience have no place in a Christian home. The ability to relax, have fun, do things together, and keep your sense of humor are powerful parenting skills.

8. *We must not verbally beat our children.* Many parents who have good intentions, under pressure, say things to their children that can destroy their confidence. Watch your tongue! Also, give your undivided attention to your child as often as you can. Always practice kindness and mercy.

9. *We must not respond irrationally when our children are in trouble.* It is tempting to defend them even when we know or suspect they may be guilty. For their sakes, we must get a grip and deal in truth and honesty. Yes, let them know you are in their comer, but allow them to suffer the painful consequences when they are guilty and in need of correction. Remember, denial hurts your children. Facing the truth is the best way to help your child, especially when dealing with drugs.

10. *Much of the pain we suffer as parents is undeserved.* But some of it is deserved and of our own making. Either way we must face it, make amends and extend forgiveness to ourselves and to others. It is the only way to peace and wholeness.

11. *There is some pain from which we need to rescue our children.* For example, if they are in schools where they are suffering, it is sometimes best to move them if you know the problem is not solvable. Let God lead you in this. Children should not be asked to bear unnecessary pain. Ask for wisdom from God.

PRESERVING A RIGHTEOUS SEED

Chapter Nine

Important Concepts in Rearing Children

What can you do to lead your children into righteousness and a disciplined, God-pleasing life?

I. *Teach your children self-control.* Self-control is necessary if they are to be "useful and fruitful" in their lives and in the knowledge of God (II Pet. 1:8). We cannot rear righteous children without teaching them self-control. It is not a popular, modem-day goal, however. II Timothy 3:1-7 talks about the last days and the difficult times to come. In verse 3, lack of self-control is listed with lovers of self and many other problems that are rampant in society today.

In the Christian life, righteousness and self-control go together. In II Peter 1:6, we see self-control listed with qualities necessary for the development of Christian virtue. In verse 9, we are told that *he who lacks these qualities is blind or shortsighted.* Verse 10 says that if we practice self-control, we will never stumble. It is one of the avenues or abundant entrances into the eternal Kingdom of God. How important it must then be to build this quality into our children.

In Galatians 5:23, self-control is listed as a fruit of the Spirit along with love and peace. In Acts 24:25-27, we find Paul discussing "righteousness, self-control, and the judgment to come." It is surprising to find self-control in between righteousness and judgment to come-major doctrines of the Christian faith.

Self-control begins with the parents who model it and then teach it to their children. We cannot expect self-control and discipline from our children when we are out of control ourselves. Children who do not learn self-control in the home will struggle with life and may never win. Many of these children grow up and take out their frustrations on their own children, perpetuating a cycle of abuse.

Anarchy in the home breeds anarchy in the community. The more children we rear who have little self-control, the more out of order our society becomes. The excess freedom used in rearing children today leads only to indulgence. Without self-control, one cannot become righteous. When we do not teach it to our children, the life of our communities suffer as well as the life of our homes. **If** you are unwilling to sacrifice your time and energy to discipline, you cannot expect self-control in your home.

2. Maintain your children's respect by conducting yourself as an adult. **If** you are a parent who shouts, screams, fights and acts like a child, you cannot expect much respect. **If** you are short-tempered, vague, preoccupied, or unloving, don't expect your relationships to thrive and be successful.

We are accountable before God for our actions. In a sense, we are accountable before our children as well. They must know who the adult is. They must be able to depend on us to be in control, which gives them physical security. We are to be understanding, which gives them emotional security. To behave maturely before them, sets a pattern of action for them to follow that is fair and demonstrates justice. Being patient with them gives them a sense of worth, importance, and value.

Important Concepts in Rearing Children

Parents should never fight with their children, striving to avoid abuse in language or action. They should not say "shut up," or slap their children across the face. If parents want the respect of their children later in life, they must respect their children now! Yes, even when they do not deserve it. We must learn to shut our mouth. We have heard so much about "good communication" that we have forgotten the virtue of guarding our mouths.

Communicate love and understanding. Give your children a sense of worth by reaching out to the best in them. Be positive and compliment them daily in constructive ways. This can work miracles in miserable, unhappy, insecure teens. Listen to them. I have spent hundreds of hours listening and sharing. It works and keeps the lines of communication open.

Choose your words carefully. Words have great impact; so, do not express to them all the negative, nasty things you think about them or their actions. This is where it is often prudent to "shut your mouth!"

Watch your volume, the tone of your voice, and even your facial expressions. Kids are smart, and they can read you like a book. Even an eyebrow raised at the wrong time can inflame them.

The familiar phrase: "Don't do as I do, but do as I say," will not work. When you are wrong or have failed to live up to the high standards God asks of us, tell your children you are sorry. But more than that ask for forgiveness. Teach your children to do the same. Set a pattern that says "Follow me, as I follow Jesus." Do not get in God's way by setting a bad example. Our aim is to rear mature godly adults. We must serve as a living example of what we want our children to be.

3. *Teach your children that true "joy" comes from God's work*

in us and is eternal, not just temporal. We must help them see that the happiness that depends on circumstances is a worldly goal. They will not understand this if you are overly ambitious for material prosperity or falling apart when adversity strikes. They must see that your joy in the Lord does not depend on what you have or don't have, or the circumstances of your life.

We don't hear a lot about instilling joy in the children we raise, and yet, we desperately need joy in our homes! The Bible has a lot to say about joy. Perhaps this oversight explains why many teens from Christian homes look to the world for what they think is joy. Read these beautiful Scriptures on joy:

> John 15:10, 11 says: *Keep My commandments. These things I have spoken to you, that My joy may be in you, and that your joy may be made full.*
>
> John 16:24 says: *Until now you have asked for nothing in My name; ask and you will receive; that your joy may be made full.*
>
> John 17: 13 says: *That they may have My joy made full in themselves.*
>
> Hebrews 12:2 says: *Fixing our eyes on Jesus, the author and peifecter of faith, who for the joy set before **Him** endured the cross, despising the shame, and has sat down at the right hand of the throne of God.*
>
> Nehemiah 8: 10 says: *The joy of the Lord is your strength.*
>
> Psalm 16:11 says: *Thou wilt make known to me the path of life; in Thy presence is fullness of joy.*
>
> Psalm 30:5 says: *For His anger is but for a moment,*

> *His favor is for a lifetime; weeping may last for the night, but a shout of joy comes in the morning.*
>
> Psalm 126:5 says: *Those who sow in tears shall reap with joyful shouting."*
>
> Psalm 132:16 says: *And her godly ones will sing aloud for joy.*
>
> Isaiah 35:10 says: *And the ransomed of the Lord will return, and come with joyful shouting to Zion, with everlasting joy upon their heads. They will find gladness and joy, and sorrow and sighing will flee away.*
>
> Romans 14:17 says: *For the kingdom of God is not eating and drinking, but righteousness and peace and joy in the Holy Spirit.*

I believe we can change our negative personalities into songs of joy in our homes. We do not have to live with the negative issues we carried with us from our growing up years, but we can develop the joy of the Lord and watch it overflow and permeate our home.

4. *Teach your children to have faith and expect great things from God.* This may mean you need to work on your own faith and confidence that God cares about your own life. True faith is a great heritage to pass on to your children. If they have seen the reality of God and the evidence of His work in your home, they are more likely to stay true to Jesus. They need to see God answering prayer and even working miracles on behalf of the family.

Our children need to understand that God does not always answer our prayers the way we expect Him to. Nevertheless, we need to trust Him because He is perfect wisdom and He loves us and knows what is best for us. He sees the whole pie-ture, not just the immediate thing we want Him to give attention to. Remembering this will keep us from becoming disillusioned and angry at God when He does not see things our way.

Let God be God! Speak His greatness! Live it before your beloved children. Your faith will grow and so will theirs.

> Deuteronomy 32:3,4 says: *Ascribe greatness to our God! The Rock! His work is perfect, for all His ways are just; a God of faithfulness and without injustice, righteous and upright is He.*

5. *Don't try to do God's work for Him.* There are some things we simply cannot do for our children. We are not smart enough to rear them without God's help, and sometimes our efforts to help Him does more harm than good. At the very least, it leaves us without peace as we seek to solve things ourselves.

If we want our children to be true believers, they must first see that we rely on God. If they see that we depend on ourselves to solve all the problems in life, they will not learn to depend on God. Our actions must say we believe and expect God to act on our behalf. Often we fail to pray, so they fail to see an expectation of the goodness of God to answer prayer. What a shame it is when we leave our children with the impression that God is nowhere around.

Some children and teens have already gotten the idea that they are too hopeless even for God. They feel that even their parents cannot handle them and have no answers for their problems and faults. As parents, we must be willing to speak hope into their lives even when we see the trauma and hardness of the situation. It is difficult to operate in faith at these times, but this is precisely the time we need to show faith the most. Our experiences from the past should tell us God is able and that He will perfect those things that concern us.

6. Do not allow your children to harbor anger. You do not want to rear a fool!

> Ecclesiastes 7:9b says: *Anger resides in the bosom of fools.*

An interesting example of this is my own grandson. Before his birth, his mother and father lived through a particularly difficult time. There also seems to be a spirit of anger that has been handed down generationally in the family. Not too many months into this baby's life, he began to aggressively fight his mother when she tried to change his diapers. He wore a big frown a lot of the time and always seemed ready for battle.

My son took hold of the situation by spanking his son and making him sit very close beside him on the sofa until the anger, the frown, and the attitude were gone. It has worked well. He has to be reminded now and then that he is frowning, but generally just a word will restore his good disposition.

Use your creative ability to solve the problem of anger in your children. Work at it. God will give you ways to help them deal with the anger. Start as soon as you see it developing. Pray fervently and don't give up. Take charge and replace their anger and misery with "joy." If you ignore it or act without hope and faith, you may indeed rear a fool.

Fathers, do not run from your responsibility to discipline. Too many men leave all the discipline to their wives. There should be unity between parents in discipline, and neither parent should "always" have to be the bad guy while the other comes off as the good parent. Actually, the parent who disciplines is the good parent.

Communication is vital when dealing with anger. A child should understand you are open to work out their problems and ready to take part of the blame for their anger if you are guilty. Not dealing with anger gives the devil an opportunity to come against you and your family.

7. *Teach your children the value of human life.* Nothing on the face of planet earth is as valuable as a human life because God wants to form all of us into His righteous seed. None of us have the right to "take life" either physically or by our words. Neither do we have the right to destroy others with criticism.

The Bible tells us God is sensitive about the opinion we have of Him and the opinions we express about Him (Job. 42:7b, 8b). It is wisdom to guard what we say about God. As a Father, He is also sensitive to the opinions we express about His other children. Yet we are constantly criticizing our brothers and sisters in Christ.

It should be easy to understand how God feels because as parents, we understand how we are affected when our children are criticized, looked down upon, or spoken of in evil ways. We know they have not "arrived" as yet, but we expect others to be understanding and patient.

Please, don't display a critical spirit in front of your children, especially with regard to other Christians. This devalues Christianity in their eyes, as well as the people we criticize. It is prudent to avoid saying hurtful things about God's other children (Prov. 12:18, Prov. 17:27, Col. 4:6, Jas. 3:2, 9,10).

8. *Teach your children to treat others in a godly manner.* My daughter told me once about listening to people describe the terrible things they endured in their homes growing up. She said, "Mom, we didn't have those problems in our home." I do not want to leave the impression we were perfect because we were not. But our children saw respect between their parents, and they were not allowed to show disrespect toward one

another. Neither were they allowed to show disrespect to adults and those in authority over them.

Small actions make small people who are small in character. Galatians 5:22-26 gives us a list of the fruit of the Spirit. Almost all of them have to do with how we treat others (love, joy, peace, patience, kindness, goodness, faithfulness, gentleness, self-control, not boastful, not challenging one another, not envying one another). These are the fruit of good relationships with others and are the very essence of Christianity.

9. *Teach your children to live selfless lives.* Selflessness is basic thoughtfulness for others with a lack of emphasis on one's self-interests. It encompasses unselfishness, thoughtfulness, and consideration for others to the point of self-sacrifice.

The theme song of this age is "self." Self-fulfillment, personal happiness at whatever cost, equal rights in every situation, personal freedom, these are repeated over and over. We must renew our minds to the thinking and expectations God has for us.

> John 15:13 says: *Greater love has no one than this, that one lay down his life for his friends.*
>
> I Thessalonians. 5: 11 says: *Encourage one another, and build up one another.*
>
> Ephesians 4:32 says: *And be kind to one another, tender-hearted, forgiving each other, just as God in Christ also has forgiven you.*

Godliness begins in the home and selflessness needs to be modeled for our children.

Children must see respect and honor for the father modeled by the mother, and they must be held accountable to respect and another. Neither were they allowed to show disrespect to adults and those in authority over them.

Small actions make small people who are small in character. Galatians 5:22-26 gives us a list of the fruit of the Spirit. Almost all of them have to do with how we treat others (love, joy, peace, patience, kindness, goodness, faithfulness, gentleness, self-control, not boastful, not challenging one another, not envying one another). These are the fruit of good relationships with others and are the very essence of Christianity.

9. *Teach your children to live selfless lives.* Selflessness is basic thoughtfulness for others with a lack of emphasis on one's self-interests. It encompasses unselfishness, thoughtfulness, and consideration for others to the point of self-sacrifice.

The theme song of this age is "self." Self-fulfillment, personal happiness at whatever cost, equal rights in every situation, personal freedom, these are repeated over and over. We must renew our minds to the thinking and expectations God has for us.

> John 15: 13 says: *Greater love has no one than this, that one lay down his life for his friends.*
>
> I Thessalonians. 5: 11 says: *Encourage one another, and build up one another.*
>
> Ephesians 4:32 says: *And be kind to one another, tender-hearted, forgiving each other, just as God in Christ also has forgiven you.*

Godliness begins in the home and selflessness needs to be modeled for our children.

Children must see respect and honor for the father modeled by the mother, and they must be held accountable to respect and obey. It is so important that children be taught to honor their fathers! If a mother fails to uphold this principle, a son will take a negative view of men in general and may not want to identify with being a man. A daughter may harden herself against ever being vulnerable to any man, seeing them as inferior beings. Out of this often comes a perversion of sexuality, resulting in confusion and role reversals.

A father must respect the mother as well, and it should be obvious to the children that he loves her. A father who does not show respect and love for his wife sets himself up for the ill will of the children. Children must be respected by the parents as well.

What does all this have to do with selfishness? It, of course, teaches our children that others are also important. Basic good manners and respect in the home prompt our children to see and meet the needs of others at the expenditure of their own efforts.

This touches another problem that is prevalent today, a lack of respect for the elderly. Read these Scriptures.

> Leviticus 19:32 says: *You shall rise up before the gray-headed, and honor the aged, and you shall revere your God, I am the Lord.*
>
> Exodus 20:12 says: *Honor your father and your mother, that your days may be prolonged in that land which the Lord your God gives you.*

10. *Teach your children not to be "takers" but "givers" in life.* Our young are notorious "takers" nowadays. We need to turn this around and teach them gratitude. We cannot expect children to develop godly unselfishness if they are reared only to seek their own way and never deny themselves anything, living self-centered lives.

Important Concepts in Rearing Children

The concept of "giving" and "self-abasement" are central to the Christian life. Just as Christ gave His life in tireless service to others on earth, and finally in death for us all, so we are called to live for others. We are to give of ourselves, our finances and the spiritual wisdom God has given us.

Children are never too young to minister to others, to put their lives into people physically, spiritually, and even financially. The Holy Spirit can really use children and young people effectively because of the purity of their spirits. Teach them to pray for people. Let them learn to serve people who come into the home.

11. *Teach your children the value of "people" over "things."* Things must be respected, but the child must know he or she is more important than the furniture, broken dishes or spilled milk.

Children need a sense of self-worth that comes from worthy actions as well as worthy character. Americans, among others, are in danger of teaching their young by their actions that materialism is the ultimate aim of life. In years now long gone, couples started married life with very few worldly possessions. They accumulated wealth over the years. Today, many young people feel they have to have "everything" to start in marriage. When they try to do this, they become so burdened with debt that they are unable to cope and the marriage flounders and often dies.

Some children are reared wearing designer clothes and are given expensive possessions and toys. No wonder they are unable to cope with life. They have never had to struggle for anything they want.

12. *Don't push the feminist agenda on your daughters.* We want our girls to be treated well. We want them to be treated

The concept of "giving" and "self-abasement" are central to the Christian life. Just as Christ gave His life in tireless service to others on earth, and finally in death for us all, so we are called to live for others. We are to give of ourselves, our finances and the spiritual wisdom God has given us.

Children are never too young to minister to others, to put their lives into people physically, spiritually, and even financially. The Holy Spirit can really use children and young people effectively because of the purity of their spirits. Teach them to pray for people. Let them learn to serve people who come into the home.

11. *Teach your children the value of "people" over "things."* Things must be respected, but the child must know he or she is more important than the furniture, broken dishes or spilled milk.

Children need a sense of self-worth that comes from worthy actions as well as worthy character. Americans, among others, are in danger of teaching their young by their actions that materialism is the ultimate aim of life. In years now long gone, couples started married life with very few worldly possessions. They accumulated wealth over the years. Today, many young people feel they have to have "everything" to start in marriage. When they try to do this, they become so burdened with debt that they are unable to cope and the marriage flounders and often dies.

Some children are reared wearing designer clothes and are given expensive possessions and toys. No wonder they are unable to cope with life. They have never had to struggle for anything they want.

12. *Don't push the feminist agenda on your daughters.* We want our girls to be treated well. We want them to be treated

justly, to learn to care for themselves in this world. If they must work outside the home, we want them to be paid fairly. We want the male authority over our girls to be wise, kind, gentle, generous, and godly.

The order of righteousness in children partly comes from a proper concept of male authority, especially "Father God" and their own father as guiding forces in their lives. If we destroy this basic foundation, we destroy the probability that they will be able to pass on a righteous heritage in their own homes. It also robs them of a basic need to feel complete.

If we teach our daughters they have to fight and battle for the basic rights of a woman, we take away their rightful peace and security. We help develop a mindset that Satan can use to say to them, "Men will always take advantage of you and do you wrong. They will not be there for you." These negative concepts can bring great unhappiness and insecurity.

I am well aware that a high percentage of men are not measuring up as fathers and leaders. This is a major problem in our culture. However, this does not give us the right as women to disregard the order God has established. Nor does it give us permission to "talk down" the father and other men in our daughters' lives. A lot depends on the mother and her ability to form godly attitudes in their children - both girls and boys. In other words, a mother can add to the problems between the sexes, and even cause perversion of sexual roles in both girls and boys.

13. *Teach your sons to be masculine (men, fathers). Teach your daughters to be feminine (women, mothers).* Satan does everything in his power to destroy the manhood of men and femininity of women.

14. *Teach your children that a sense of accomplishment is desirable and gives a feeling of satisfaction from a job well*

done. Accomplishments can be a warm blanket against the coldness of life. It can protect our children from feeling inferior, insecure, or worthless. Find their God-given interests and talents (inside godliness) and help them develop those. Give them something to work with. It may be as simple as paper and crayons. Encourage them to learn by letting them help you. Share your knowledge.

Let your children experience what a good feeling they get from bringing cleanliness and order out of disorder. Start teaching them early to clean up the messes they make. Help them by setting an example, show them how to work, and encourage them when the task is a big one. They need responsibility starting at an early age. The more varied a child's experience, the more he or she will bring into the lives of those close to him or her, and the more self-confidence he or she will attain.

Before I go any further, let me say that pride can be a terrible problem. If it becomes unbalanced or a cover up for inferiority or insecurity, it can be counterproductive. We try to protect ourselves by our pride. Be aware if you see that pride is becoming a "crutch" for your child.

There are two areas I especially want to mention. The first is manners. "Rude and crude" is the atmosphere in a lot of homes today, and it is reinforced by television. Families rarely or never meet together for a formal meal, and children enter the adult world with little idea how to behave in social situations. Please do not send your child out into a hostile world unsure of how to use their dining instruments.

We had a little game we played with our children at Sunday lunch. Any child, caught by a peer, with elbows on the table or other breech of etiquette had to leave the room and count to 100 before returning to the table. The one with the best manners was given a little money.

PRESERVING A RIGHTEOUS SEED

Teach your children how to set the table properly. They may never need to know, but if they are thrust into society without knowing, they may feel nervous and insecure. I've seen the young teased or ridiculed because they did not know how to use their knives.

Mothers, please teach your daughters to cook. Our culture today just does not leave much time for such things. Many girls know little about this before marriage. But it is important that they become proficient in the area of nutrition. The health of our nation depends on mothers who know how to put together a healthy meal.

When our four boys were growing up, we allowed them to experiment in my kitchen. They concocted some interesting dishes. For instance, we once had enchiladas that were colored green with food coloring. And once they tried to make doce-de-leite, a Brazilian treat. A can of Eagle Brand condensed milk is boiled, totally submerged in water, for two hours until it becomes a soft caramel. Good stuff! Only this particular time they went off to play. They let the all the water boil out and the can exploded covering everything, including the ceiling.

15. *Teach your children the concept of service to others.* It is not demeaning to serve others. Jesus taught and ministered to people constantly. But our society has become so warped that we feel that we must be in charge or we are not a success in life.

16. *Teach your children to love the Bible and read it.* Let them see you reading your Bible and that you give your time to it often. We don't usually like to do this when the children are around. Their presence can be distracting making it hard to concentrate. They may bump or tear our nice Bible or accidentally pull out a page. But taking the time and making that extra effort makes a valuable memory they will not forget.

In the early '50s, we got our first television in my parents' home. I was around seventeen years old and my two brothers were younger. My father was a Bible teacher and usually studied in his bedroom. But after the arrival of the television, he often came to his bedroom door to see what we were watching. He felt it could not be trusted, and he was proven right. But I can still see him standing in that doorway for just a few minutes at a time with his open Bible in his hands. It made a lasting mental picture that I have not forgotten in 50 years.

We even stooped to giving money for long Bible passages our children learned to quote. Memorizing Psalm 91 was required of each child, and we repeated it together as a family in the mornings for years before we separated for the day. We still do this sometimes when we are together. It is rewarding to hear them quoting the Bible years later. You can do it! You will not be sorry!

Finally, God is still working in your children's lives, just as He is still working in yours! Your children are not fully mature yet, so let the grace of God be in you as you attempt to teach them godly living in this world.

PRESERVING A RIGHTEOUS SEED

Chapter Ten

False Concepts Under Which We Raise Our Children

There are false concepts our society has developed that we allow to prevail, and because of them, our children grow up confused. Let's look at some of these false concepts.

I. *We have a false concept of who God is and what He requires from us.* This generation has come to see God as a big "sugar daddy" who meets our needs if He wants to and turns His back on us if we displease Him. Others see Him as just a big "softy" who loves everyone, no matter how they live. He just loves, loves, loves, and forgives, forgives, forgives.

Both of these concepts reduce God to an emotional rather than rational Being. The truth is that He is both emotional and rational, and we are created in His image. The Bible gives examples of God's emotions: anger, revenge, pain, and hate. Do you find it difficult to believe that God can feel such negative emotions? If so, remember that His emotions and actions always come out of righteousness. In other words, God experiences righteous anger, righteous revenge, and hatred of lawlessness. These are not feelings that come from the basic depravity of mankind.

The rational side of God sees our rebellion, our ugly moods, our stubbornness, our deliberate disobedience, our lack of

PRESERVING A RIGHTEOUS SEED

love. He understands all the reasons and circumstances prompting such behavior, but He requires us to rise above these feelings and to react rationally. We will then be able to correct our stubborn, rebellious, hateful ways. God is love, but He can also be severe.

> Romans 11:22 says: *Behold then the kindness and severity of God; to those who fell, severity, but to you, God's kindness, if you continue in His kindness; otherwise you also will be cut off.*

If we love our children, we will walk in kindness toward them. But if they resist our kindness, then we must be prepared to use severity for the sake of their very souls. We serve a balanced God; He is great in mercy, but He is not overboard. He does not "wink" at our sins. We are accountable, whether we think so or not. God is not a permissive father! He is a Father Who always disciplines with wisdom, understanding, patience, and love. He is never blinded by His emotions, nor does He discipline us recklessly. His emotions are never out of control.

If we have true love for our children, we will not be permissive because it is not in their best interest and could even destroy them.

> Proverbs 3:12 says: *For whom the LORD loves He reproves, even as a father, the son in whom he delights.*

Let me point out three biblical examples of parents who were permissive. Two of them were priests and the other a king. They were great men of God, but failed miserably as fathers.

Eli, the great high priest of Israel, had sons who *"lay with the women who served at the doorway of the tent of meeting"*(I Samuel 2:22). They committed fornication with the women who served. Verse 12 says, *"The sons of Eli were worthless men; who did not know the LORD."* Eli warned them, but they did not listen. He apparently honored his sons above God because he did not take the necessary steps to stop them from committing such hideous sins. Eli also made himself fat from the *"choicest of every offering of My people Israel"* (I Samuel 2:29).

> God spoke in I Samuel 2:30 saying, *For those who honor Me I will honor, and those who despise Me will be lightly esteemed.*

Eli was judged for the *"iniquity which he knew"* in his sons, and God said their sins *"shall not be atoned for by sacrifice or offerings forever"* (I Samuel 3:13,14).

Samuel was a high priest and great spiritual leader. He was an upright judge, who was consecrated to God and heard His voice. He was courageous and a man of prayer, an inspired prophet, and a circuit judge. I Samuel 8:3-5 says, *"His sons... did not walk in his ways, but turned aside after dishonest gain and took bribes and perverted justice."* Samuel was a godly priest, but his sons were not.

King David was beautiful in appearance and a man after God's own heart. He was a poet, divinely chosen for God's purpose, and courageous. He was also a great soldier and a champion. Two of his sons, Absalom and Adonijab, tried to take the kingdom from their father. The Bible tells us in I Kings 1:6, that Adonijab exalted himself and that his father (David) had never crossed him, asking *"why have you done so?"*

> Proverbs 29:15 says: *"The rod and reproof give wisdom, but a child who gets his own way brings shame to his mother."*

Our God is a God of kindness and severity, not just blind love that overlooks our sins. When He looks at us, He sees us in the light of eternity. In fact, even the things that make us happy are seen by Him in an eternal perspective. His desire is for our eternal joy, not just our temporal happiness. The joy of the Lord is mentioned often in the Bible, but interestingly, there is no mention of the personal happiness we spend our lives pursuing. He is not hesitant to make us unhappy on earth if it will bring about our eternal good.

> Deuteronomy 32:3,4 says: *He is a God of faithfulness. His work is perfect. All His ways are just. He is without injustice. He is righteous and upright always.*

2. *We have a false concept of love, especially God's love.* Today, love is seen, first of all, as a feeling. This implies an exaggerated sense of self-interest. Without righteousness and covenant relationship, love takes many shapes: "Make me happy!" "Fulfill my needs!" "Make me feel good!" All is sacrificed to satisfy our feelings-what we want.

Television has defined love for us, but it is a perverted, irresponsible love. Basically, it says, "Love is sex-any kind and by any means is acceptable." Our children watch this idea pushed daily on television, and they accept it because there is so little biblical teaching to counteract it in our homes.

And consider this. Simply taking your children to church will not secure them morally if you fail to challenge the concepts they see on television. The morals of many children who were raised in church are as bad as those of the world. You simply cannot allow the television to baby-sit your children just to give yourself a little peace.

Ungodly friends can also lead your children astray. A bond formed with this kind of friend can bring about a stubborn and dangerous loyalty. Sometimes children bring "another spirit" into your home when they have been visiting friends. That spirit can rise up in your children. It's easy to let things slide, but do not ignore it-deal with it!

The ultimate example of love was Jesus as He lived for others and ultimately died on the cross for us. I Corinthians 13 basically says we can be very religious, have many spiritual gifts, be able to sway crowds with our words, have a lot of faith, be extremely benevolent, even give ourselves in martyrdom and still not have love. And without love, all those things would profit us nothing. That should scare us to death! So much of the modern church is hung up right here.

WHAT IS LOVE?

I Corinthians 13 tells us that love is patient, kind, not jealous, does not brag, is not arrogant, does not act unbecomingly, does not look out just for self, refuses to be provoked, does not take into account wrongs suffered, does not rejoice (or enjoy) unrighteousness but rejoices in truth, bears all things, believes, hopes, endures. Prophecy, tongues and knowledge will end but love will never end. Love is the greatest part of our faith, and it will always exist and always be the foundation of our eternal life.

The product of love should be righteousness, rather than self-fulfillment. True love involves faithfulness and commitment, even as God is faithful and committed. It involves loving-kindness and comes through covenant relationship and responsibility. Love demands that we learn sacrifice, character, commitment, selflessness, purpose, order, righteousness, and concern for others.

A child who is reared according to the humanistic view of life, where ME is at the center of everything, will have severe problems in life and may ultimately miss a wonderful eternity with God. Yes, we do have a great responsibility when we have brought children into the world.

3. *We "are" our feelings.* This premise says that "we should do whatever feels good." We choose to submit ourselves to our feelings. Many spend most of their lives under the tyranny of their feelings.

Catherine Marshall, in her book *Beyond Ourselves,* wrote of her experience with emotions and will. "Our emotions are not the real us. The motivating force at the center of our physical being is our will. The dictionary describes 'will' as 'the power of conscious, deliberate action.' The will is the governing power in us, the rudder, the spring of all our actions" *(Beyond Ourselves* by Catherine Marshall, McGraw Hill, New York, 1961, pg. 58).

The outstanding function of the human spirit is "choosing." If your will is not free to choose, you are in trouble. On page 56 of the book, *Beyond Ourselves,* Catherine also correctly points out that the Christian life must be lived in the will, not in the emotions. God regards the decisions and choices of a man's will as the decisions and choices of a man himself, no matter how contrary his emotions may be.

My husband often says, "Righteous desires make you righteous, unrighteous desires make you unrighteous." All of us are tempted with evil, but it is our will that determines whether our bad desires will rule us or not. With our will, we can choose to be righteous.

Children must be taught that we are not our feelings. It is our will that must conform to God's will. Left unchecked, our feelings entrap us in the "victim mentality," a concept that has overpowered and warped our culture. If our feelings are stomped on or we are damaged in any way, we feel we are victims. God deals with our wills, not so much our feelings. We must get this across to our children, or they will live their lives on a superficial level.

Who is the highest power in your world; you or God? If we are under God's control, we function well. If we are self-willed, we are in bondage to ourselves. When we are on the throne of our lives, we fight God at every turn, believing our ways are the right ways. When God is dethroned, we are on our own.

Relying on feelings is a problem in the Church as well. If we are stirred in our feelings, we believe it was a good service. But nothing in us really changes until our "will" makes a change in us.

4. Kids have the right to make their own choices without our interference. The problem with this is that children do not have the wisdom, maturity, focus or understanding to make some decisions. Yes, they have to learn to stand on their own two feet and to make their decisions, but they must have the benefit of what we have learned. That is our job, our responsibility. All we need to do is ask God Who is generous in giving us wisdom.

> James 1:5 says: *But if any of you lacks wisdom, let him ask of God, who gives to all men generously and without reproach and it will be given to him.*

If we ask in faith, God will guide us in teaching our children to make wise decisions. We must pray and rely on the Spirit of God to reveal truth to our children, and we must trust Him also to give them a receptive heart to walk in the truth.

There is a time to release the child to make decisions. This comes gradually and happens more often as they mature. This is not generally for small children. Small children require more disciplined structure. Don't let the world tell you that you are forcing your child into an undesirable mold. Righteous seeds need establishing (planting), cultivating (watering and weeding), and time to grow. Then they will mature well and be ready for their future.

5. *Spanking or inflicting pain on a child is child abuse and teaches aggression.* Beating a child, or verbally lashing out at them with abusive language from our own frustrations and bad disposition is certainly child abuse. But inflicting a certain amount of pain to break their stubborn self-will is biblical.

Pain inflicted by a loving, righteous parent brings healing to the soul and breaks the power of rebellion. However, it must be administered in justice, calmness, self-control, and with enough force to get the desired results.

If your child responds to discipline without force, that is great. But most children require some pain before they can be molded into God's model. After disciplining our children, it is imperative that we learn to bring them into a spirit of peace and reconciliation, which of course is the spirit of Christ.

Some of you reading this have so bought into the philosophy of the world that you will insist on misunderstanding these statements. It is true that discipline given in an undisciplined manner may do more harm than good. But God has placed His approval on pain because He knows the extent of our unbending nature and that few of us will truly become what we should without being forced there by pain.

We are often self-centered little children at heart who want our own way and live for self-gratification. How sad! The supposed problem of aggression coming out of spanking is backward. Spanking is the breaking of a rebellious spirit or a spirit that will not bend to authority. John Wesley said, "Constant obedience is the aim of our life toward God." And this is what we want our children to learn.

6. *A child needs freedom to develop properly.* It is a misconception that a child has a right to freedom without boundaries. The concept of freedom includes boundaries, structure, and

limitations. There is order in God's creation, and freedom without limitations is an illusion.

Both the Old and New Testaments support this truth. In the Garden of Eden, Adam and Eve were not allowed to eat of the tree of good and evil and God set boundaries for the Children of Israel when he gave the Ten Commandments to Moses. Those same laws were still in place in the New Testament, but because of the grace of God extended to us through Jesus Christ they are perfected.

God even limits Himself through His own holiness. Limiting ourselves and accepting those limits to our freedom, is a Kingdom principle. We must teach restraint and limits to our children if we want to see them lead happy, peaceful, and contented lives.

True freedom is being content to fulfill God's purposes, His righteousness, and not our own. Man without limitations and structure is like a building without a proper framework; it will not stand. It will self-destruct, and so will a man (or child) who has no structure in his life.

The world's concept of freedom is reflected in the dictionary definition: "Freedom is basically being unrestricted. It is the condition of being exempt from or not subject to certain things. Freedom is self-determination and self-direction."

There are also many words that have both good and bad implications because they are "power" words. Basically, "power" is the bottom line in our discussion regarding children. Who should demonstrate power over a child? Himself or his parents? A few of these words are: unconstrained, boldness, audacity, forwardness, brazenness, impertinence, impudence, disrespect, arrogance, presumption, brass, nerve, exemption, immunity, liberation, deliverance, independence, license, frankness, outspokenness, undue familiarity, freedom to act, taking liberty or the right to liberty in all things.

These words are all used to describe some form or aspect of freedom. As you can see, many of the words have terrible implications for our children. Most imply an attitude of self-centeredness that does not bring freedom. It binds us to ourselves and sometimes makes us introverted, rather than God conscious or God pleasing. It is an attitude that spawns "agendas" and "causes." We become bound by indulgences, greed, and lusts, losing our sense of purpose and destiny.

Children should not be allowed to rule the home by tyranny. They should not be allowed to be rude or crude. These are not rights or freedoms that belong to children. Yet homes are being destroyed in this way. Some parents are completely controlled by the tyranny and bad manners of their children. Children must be made to understand from the beginning of their lives that freedom is not absolute. Others have rights and feelings also. They must know that when they violate the rules of the home or society, they lose the freedom they imagine they have.

The very worst part of this independent, self-centered spirit is that those who indulge it can never be truly spiritual because they are resisting the very foundation of God's order. The focus of salvation is man's "will," that is, man freely choosing to do God's will. Those who are bound to themselves have literally lost their ability to choose God's way. True freedom is having your will bonded to the will of God. The "spirit of independence" that is permeating our families today creates blind spots in our perceptions. Things are not seen as a whole but from a biased, self-centered point of view.

SO WHAT FREEDOM AND RIGHTS DOES A CHILD HAVE?

It takes time and energy, plus creativity, to form righteous character in a child! Some parents are unwilling or cannot focus their attention on the job of guiding the life of their children. But our children have the right to our time. They have the right to both quality and quantity time. They have the right to our hearts. They have the right to our wholehearted effort to be a godly parent. They have a right to our love, unfailingly, without undue or undeserved anger, resentment, or impatience. They have the right to expect us to be there for the long haul. ... They have a right to expect us to lead them into the truth of God. They have the right to freedom from abuse at our hands.

When children are given false freedom but do not receive what God says they are entitled to, there is often the definite formation of self-will, self-importance, and self-indulgence. It comes because we have not properly trained them, and often develops as a by-product or a defense against neglect. False freedom does not bring happiness.

7. *We must extend mercy, and let our children go free from all offenses.* Mercy is a valid virtue. God is full of mercy and extends that mercy to us when we are repentant and seeking Him. But there is a "false mercy" that fails to call sin into account. Sin becomes covered over by this false mercy, and it is never dealt with.

Children must learn to call sin, sin! This is a major problem in our world today and ties in with our wrong concept of love. We have been convinced (almost brainwashed) into thinking it is not love to be strict with or inflict pain on our children when disciplining them. We fail to take into account that God inflicts pain and chastises us as dear children to mold us for the Kingdom of God.

> Deuteronomy 8:5 says: *Thus you are to know in your heart that the **LORD** your God was disciplining you just as a man disciplines his son.*

> Psalm 94:12 says: *Blessed is the man whom Thou dost chasten, O LORD, and dost teach out of Thy law.*
>
> Proverbs 3:11 says: *My son, do not reject the discipline of the LORD, or loathe His reproof.*
>
> Proverbs 3:12 says: *For whom the LORD loves He reproves, even as a father, the son in whom he delights.*
>
> Revelation 3:19 says: *Those whom I love, I reprove and discipline; be zealous therefore, and repent.*

Since God uses this means with us, it makes sense that we should use the same means with our children. By all means have mercy! To have mercy is to be "like God." But, hold your children accountable for their unrighteous conduct and sins. This also is "like God." Do not make excuses or blindly defend a child who gets into trouble. You cannot preserve a righteous seed by failing to discipline.

8. *If a child experiences enough love, your children will turn out well.* Many parents adhere to this philosophy and expect every meaningful, worthwhile virtue to spring forth spontaneously. This premise is humanistic in nature and contrary to the Word of God.

Love is extremely important! I have no quarrel with loving a child. I doubt you can love a child too much, but I do believe you can love them unwisely. Love alone is not sufficient to form righteousness in children, nor does it produce character. Only godly discipline produces godly character. Without the discipline, they become selfish, self-indulgent, deceitful and despise their elders.

Parents who do not love and discipline their children are putting them at great risk and handicapping them for life. How can children be whole when they perceive their very source of life-their parents-do not love them enough to guide them and set boundaries for them?

9. *Young people have the answers; therefore, the elders should move over and let the young run things.*

From this premise comes the exaggerated emphasis on youthful looks, clothing, pursuits, even knowledge. The basic feeling here is that anything new is always better than the old; therefore, the old is rejected. Out of this comes the idea that "all change is good." In fact, the idea that "time brings change" and "all change is good" is the basic theory of evolution.

It is a great deception in our day that through time, man is developing and realizing an ever onward and upward progression. Many history teachers believe that history is ever progressing, developing stage by stage through time to perfection. In this view, history loses its meaning, events of the past are unimportant because they are only a part of the progression.

Tradition is rejected, and elders are not respected, listened to, or sought out for counsel. Nothing is considered evil in itself. Violence is viewed as part of the natural progression of things. We are urged not to inhibit our children or require them to conform. This, of course, is not the Christian view. We believe there was a beginning and there will be an end. In between there is "providence," the protective care of God. Looking for "time" to solve all problems is a philosophy for those who do not believe in God.

As for youth, "theirs" is a position of vulnerability. They have tremendous energy, enthusiasm, and impetuousness. They are prone to take up causes and force things to happen. But they are also prone to failure. They fall apart emotionally and are definitely hindered by their lack of life experience. They are idealistic, wanting to solve the problems of the world without having solved their own problems.

The battle here is between Christianity and humanism. Humanism looks for answers to our problems in a human way, human answers. Christianity looks to a divine or supernatural God for answers.

10. *What you own and are able to produce determines your self worth.* Those who adhere to this premise find that spiritual matters and righteous character are devalued in comparison to the value of worldly possessions. In other words, what you wear, the kind of car you drive, the size and beauty of your home, what you have achieved, tells the world how valuable you are as a person and establishes in your own mind your self-worth. This is materialism, and it leads to pride, arrogance and an un-Christlike attitude of superiority.

Certainly, we need clothes to wear, comfortable homes in which to dwell, and work that is worthwhile and fulfilling with eternal value; but beyond that, we need to learn to give of all we have and are. Children who are reared under godly concepts of giving do not fall as easily into the rat race of materialism and the destructive pattern of failure and loss of worth that the lack of material prosperity brings.

Chapter Eleven

Concepts that Destroy Order in the Home

God operates out of order and truth, and these principles should guide us as we strive to imitate Christ. Order and truth should permeate our homes. If we buy into the world's customs and values, we are sure to lose that order and we will no longer operate from a foundation of truth.

There is great battle today to replace God's order of authority for the home. We should know and understand the false concepts that are emerging in this holy war. They are not truth, but are presented to society as truth. Consider these:

1. It is good for women to be free from male authority. This starts in the home and is reinforced by society. One of the greatest gifts we can give our children is to teach them to respect authority, especially the authority of their fathers. This is to be modeled for them first by their mothers.

If respect is not shown and there is bitterness against men, the general seeds of insurrection and chaos will be passed on from generation to generation. Daughters will be unable to establish healthy homes. Sons will be unable to feel any pride in their manhood and function as the heads of their homes.

Bitter women rear bitter daughters because "children learn

what they live." Domineering, strong-willed women, full of hurts and rejection do not bring forth children formed in righteousness. When a woman fails to accept headship and authority, she often operates out of a spirit of pride, control, and witchcraft. There is a perverted sense of satisfaction and superiority in holding the controlling power.

One of the major problems is the misuse of power in the area of sex. Many men are in bondage to their lusts and many women fuel that fire by their sexual seductions. Women complain bitterly about sexual harassment, yet continue to dress provocatively. Sex has become the foundation of the twentieth-century society and the driving force behind so much of our culture.

The use of sex to manipulate is called witchcraft. If you look up the meaning of the word, you will see that its main root meaning is witchery and has to do with fascinating girls or women, who exercise power through their beauty and enchantments. I Peter 3:2-5, provides counsel for women regarding how they should dress.

2. *There is an onslaught against the position of men.* This attack does not allow boys to grow up with a healthy understanding of what God accepts as a man's position in the world.

John Leo, who writes especially about social problems for *U.S. News and World Report,* had this to say in the May 11, 1998, issue: "But the worst impact of all the male bashing is on the young."

Barbara Wilder Smith, a teacher and researcher in the Boston area, was recently quoted in several newspapers on how deeply anti-male attitudes have affected the schools. When she made 'Boys Are Good' T-shirts for boys in her class, all 10 of the female student-teachers under her supervision objected to the message. (One, she said, was wearing a button saying, 'So many men, so little intelligence.') "My son can't even wear the shirt out in his backyard," she said. "People see it and object strongly and shout things."

"On the other hand," she says, "nobody objects when girls wear shirts that say 'Girls Rule' or when they taunt the boys with the chant, 'Boys go to Jupiter to get more stupider; girls go to college to get more knowledge.' Worse, many adolescent boys object to the 'Boys Are Good' shirts, too, because they have come to accept the cultural messages that something is seriously wrong with being male."

These comments help us understand the effect feminism and society have had on the attitude of women toward men, especially in the case of the young. Tolerating men for the purpose of using them to father our children or provide for our material needs is decidedly "not Christian." God requires that women respect the men in their lives. Fathers are important. They provide an example of manliness in our sons lives, and give identity to both sons and daughters.

Unfortunately, fatherlessness is the crisis of our day. Mothers who are left to raise their sons alone often produce men who are dependent on women or confused concerning their male identities. They need fathers to pattern their lives after. A good percentage of homosexual problems can be traced to this. I have noticed that as feminism has taken more and more control in our society so has the problem of homosexuality.

It's true that men sometimes exhibit an overbearing, even abusive, attitude toward women. It is not easy to wield authority with humility. Some men have not even tried, and this has caused many women to rebel. Men who operate out of an exaggerated sense of arrogant male superiority are not demonstrating Christian character. Such conduct defies all the biblical instructions concerning how Christians should act toward each other. Study the fruit of the Spirit in Galatians 5:22 for an example of Christian character.

God does not operate arrogantly toward us and neither should husbands and fathers operate toward wives and children in this way. God always judges arrogance, and He will judge a man who blindly and unjustly uses this kind of perverted authority. Authority should operate out of love and concern for the other person, just as God's authority operates out of His love for us.

3. *The greatest area of chaos in the home today comes from children who have been reared to believe they are the center of the universe and everyone and everything exists for them and revolves around them.* These children basically hold their parents hostage and anarchy rules their lives and the lives of those around them. By our own actions, we cause small children to believe this and they grow up incredibly self-centered.

We are probably the first generation of parents who are afraid of our own children. We are afraid to take a stand against the accepted, popular thought of the day. We are afraid to discipline, and sometimes, we are physically afraid of them. We are afraid that our children will not like us or consider us a friend. Friendship is good, but it is more important to be a godly parent.

Some parents must sleep with their bedroom doors locked because they know they are harboring violent children, filled with anger, hate, and revenge. Some of these children, especially adopted ones from some foreign countries, feel so destroyed, so abandoned, and unwanted they react in total frustration and violence against others and themselves. This is known as Attachment Disorder Syndrome and these children are so disturbed that they are filled with self-hatred and constantly in danger of hurting themselves and others. These children truly are victims, but become predators because of the feelings of abandonment that have formed the core of their being.

Concepts that Destroy Order in the Home

Many children are formed in a vacuum. That is, no one really focuses on their needs. Control is lost with some of our children at a very early age.

4. *Children who are taught that their "rights" are absolute are on their way to being totally self-centered.* Teach your children the virtue of justice rather than self-centered rights. God is just. When we teach our children that justice is a virtue, we make it easier for them to understand why our "rights" must be tempered with concern for the welfare of others. We must teach our children to live justly.

> Zephaniah 3:5 says: *The Lord is righteous within her, He will do no injustice. Every morning He brings His justice to light; He does not fail.* We must not fail our children.

5. *Equality no matter the cost and whatever cause has become the goal of our society, our homes, and our churches.* We need to recognize that dying to self and all selfish ambition is a trait of those who will inherit the kingdom of God. We cannot teach Bible principles and make a crusade of equal rights as a standard in our homes.

There is a measure of equality in the Gospel that says "whosoever will may come" to the cross for salvation. But equality is not a biblical principle. That may sound like a shocking statement to you, but if you will think and study you will see this is true.

If equality had been an issue with Jesus, He would have made a crusade of freeing all slaves. Instead He taught them how to live as slaves. He did not make the servant equal with his master. I am not saying He approved of slavery, I am just saying He made no real issue as far as equality was concerned.

Teaching children that spiritual rewards for what they give are the things they can live with and feel good about helps them develop godly character.

6. *Tolerance is a concept that the world espouses daily.* The television is the main purveyor of this concept and it seems to apply to everything except Christianity. The world has no tolerance for Christians nor their principles. They are branded "bigots" when they stand for what they believe.

Tolerance allows children to develop in their own way and says that we, as a society accept anything. It incorporates open-mindedness, broad-mindedness, permissiveness, indulgence, lenience. It tells us to forgive everything, be easygoing and big-hearted, and turn a blind eye. One glimpse at this list given for the word tolerance should be enough to convince us it is not a biblical concept and should not be a tenant of childrearing. We need strong backbones to be good parents. When God said "You shall not," He meant "Don't do it!"

7. *The victim mentality has warped our sense of justice, caused chaos, and destroyed order in the home.* Some truly are victims, especially those innocent and vulnerable children who are scarred by abuse. Even babies in the womb can be victimized. Sometimes these small victims can only be brought right by prayer and fasting or the intervention of someone who understands and is anointed in the deliverance ministry.

However, the devil can build strongholds in your children when they are allowed to focus in a "poor me" mentality. Do not allow your children to see themselves this way or take this attitude in life.

There is a sense of compassion for victims in our society. The problem is that many people have taken this too far and are now using their identification as a "victim" to avoid taking responsibility for their actions, shifting blame and fault for their failures to others or to their circumstances. Compassion sense is always in order. It is an attribute of God, but it must be yoked with commonsense.

If you are a victim yourself, do not allow your hurts to color the thinking of your children. As a parent, do not indulge in self-pity, snide remarks or bad attitudes. Your children are sure to pick-up on these things and carry them over into their lives. Set an example for your children by acting as a person whose life has been redeemed by Christ. Be encouraging, uplifting, and positive. Negative attitudes reinforce the victim mentality.

Stop examining your life and going from person to person, ministry to ministry, telling your life story. Go to God for help, for our help comes from the Lord who made heaven and earth. Your problems are not too difficult for Him. Allow Him to heal you. Jesus came to set the captive free and His healing of the negative things that have molded your life and character are every bit as real and amazing as the healing of physical cancer. Jesus is always the answer.

8. The spirit of independence that has permeated our society destroys the unity and order of the home. Teach your children to be capable and qualified for life, but not independent in the areas of need and association of people. We all need others and this need was created in us by God Himself to keep us from being isolated and alone in this life.

For the most part, people who shut others out of their lives and have become completely self-sufficient are miserable. This is a very real problem among our young people. Isolation has caused them to have trouble communicating. This is not a good way to go through life.

Christianity as well as Judaism are communal religions. This means they function for the good of the whole community and the individual. They seek the good of others. This requires a serving, self-sacrificial life. Idolatry, on the other hand, is loving anything more than Jesus Christ. This applies to loving yourself too much and manifests itself in an independent spirit.

Men who feel they have a right to do what they want, who think of themselves first and foremost, fail to understand or care about the unity of the home and marriage. There has to be a certain amount of unity and togetherness in a home for it to function properly.

Women who have declared their independence rob the home of the nurturing it needs. They move from the spirit of Christianity to the spirit of idolatry. That means they love themselves more than they love the unity and godliness God ordained for the home. Independence often leads to idolatry, which results in love of self more than love for others.

Children who are nurtured by an independent spirit have little chance to be a righteous seed. They develop the same self-centered ways as their parents.

9. *An entertainment mentality has taken over our homes.* This is not news to most Christians. It is the reason behind a lot of the passivity in parents and the inability of children to be at peace. There seems to be a restlessness in the spirit of most children today, and many parents feel they must furnish entertainment for all their children's waking moments.

A child should not be encouraged to build a world of his or her own, separate and apart from the family. Through friends, television, video games, computers, and computer games, children have the ability to escape into a separate world. The maturing child needs to learn to communicate and relate to others.

Children who are isolated through computers or television also run the risk of becoming emotionally cold and lonely and may acquire a feeling of unreality, and disconnectedness. These problems open the door for drugs and with drugs come spaciousness, escapism and sometimes open doors into an adult world that is far beyond a child's need to know.

The games for both computers and television are so fast paced that they often create a tension in a child that makes it difficult for them to relax or settle down to ordinary life. In a child's life, there should be time for creativity, contemplation, dreaming, thinking about the deep meaning of life, and connecting with God.

Parents are wise to control the computer and television. I suggest they be used only in a central room, with time limits for each family member. Children who learn discipline and limits in the home will be better able to set realistic limits and discipline themselves.

This is probably the first time in history man has been so disconnected from reality. Big cities help create this unreality, and our "hurry up" culture drives people into isolation, panic, even rage. Without a daily connection with the wonders of God's creation, they become disconnected from life. Many city children are reared in apartments and never see a beautiful sunrise or sunset. They have never been conscious of the birds singing. Often they have not had the opportunity to experience the miracle of birth, even that of a kitten.

All in all, they have a totally distorted picture of life and what God's eternal values are. I want to repeat a phrase here I hope you will get into your spirit and work from, "Don't allow anything in your home that you do not want your children to love." Satan will take advantage of any small footholds he can get, and use it to destroy your child.

I hope these thoughts will help you understand why the home is in such chaos today, and why our children are in such trouble. From my vantage point, I can tell you things have not always been as they are now. You, as parents, are dealing with problems that were not even dreamed of when you were children. But the same God exists! He is full of wisdom and compassion for those who love Him and seek His help!

Chapter Twelve

Teen Suicide and Violence

Suicide among young people has nearly tripled since the 1950s. It has become the third leading cause of death among teens, falling behind accidents and homicides. These statistics send a desperate message. Most children and teens probably do not really mean to die. Some no doubt do not even understand what dying means. They simply find themselves in so much pain mentally that they can no longer cope.

The highest number of suicides happen during summer months, rather than in December as is commonly thought. In recent years, copycat suicides in the schools have become a common occurrence. Although the tendency is not inherited, there is a higher risk in families and schools where someone has committed suicide.

An estimated 750,000 to 1,000,000 people attempt to kill themselves in the U.S. each year. Some 30 to 40 thousand succeed. These are not all adults or teens, 3 to 11 year olds are included in these statistics.

SUICIDE

What elements in a child's life would bring him or her to the point of suicide?

1. *Depression from the loss of father or mother through divorce or death can produce a sense of isolation and hopelessness.*

PRESERVING A RIGHTEOUS SEED

2. *Fighting between parents and general instability in the home can bring severe emotional pain.*

3. *The breakdown of communication can create an emptiness and sense of isolation.*

4. *Expectations placed on children can make them feel hopeless.* This can include academic expectations or just perfectionism coming through a father or mother. It can also operate out of their own life causing them to be unable to accept any flaws or failures in themselves.

5. *Conflict between what parents teach and expect and the pressure of peers can pull them in opposite directions to the point of desperation.*

6. *Inconsistency in parents between what they believe and what they practice can create internal conflict.*

7. *A sense that they have disappointed those they love can create unbearable pain and guilt.*

8. *Drug addictions and the fear of being found out can cause a sense of hopelessness.* Some cannot bear knowing that they will disappoint the people they love and themselves as well.

9. *Rejection coming from a young love is a common cause of teen suicide.*

10. *Rejection from peers may well be the second leading cause of suicide in teens.* It certainly is a major cause.

11. *Depression coming from physical problems or inherited through the genes can become overwhelming.*

12. *Sensitive young people can be totally destroyed by the ugliness, injustice, pain and suffering in the world.* This is sometimes part of the pain behind anorexia and bulimia.

13. *An unsuccessful search for real love can set up a feeling of hopelessness.* This failure often comes out of the home. Some people are born with a feeling of rejection and abandonment. They are unable to believe anyone can love them.

14. *Alcohol and drug abuse can induce an irrationality and lack of judgment that sometimes results in accidental or deliberate suicide.*

15. *Perverted fantasies can cause a break with reality.* Children whose whole lives are wrapped up in or focused on television, videos, and computer games often develop a perverted sense of reality. They no longer know what is important and real and what is fantasy. Sources of these perverted fantasies are movies, television, revenge fantasies, occult games such as Dungeon and Dragons, death, terror, and anything that takes away from the reality of God can open the door for Satan to come into our children's lives and destroy them.

16. *Rock music with such titles such as "Don't Fear the Reaper" and lyrics glorifying death, or the infliction of pain, can penetrate the subconscious with messages of suicide.* The rock beat is agitating to the nervous system. The rhythm breaks down control and inhibitions causing teenagers to commit acts that destroy their standards of righteousness.

Guard your children's hearts, ears, and spirits. Make sure the things they are doing are things that will build them up, rather than destroy their lives and personalities. I say again, "Don't allow in your home anything that you don't want your children to love."

VIOLENCE

Violence coming from angry kids is on the increase. It is the result of a failure to meet the basic needs of a child. Being rejected, abandoned, even despised and made fun of, can cause violence to enter the heart of the child. Receiving rejection from their peers can cause them to feel inferior and destroy the image they have of themselves. This often induces deep anger and feelings of worthlessness. This is probably not a form of insanity, but it works itself out as irrationality.

Children who are bullied, teased, and tormented by others with no respect for their person or humanness can build up an unbelievable amount of hostility. Children are often tormented and picked on because they wear glasses or look different. Sometimes, they are called names such as nerd, dweeb, or fatso. A person treated in this manner is capable of picking up a gun as an equalizer or a way of revenge. They sometimes shoot or stab their parents before going on a rampage of killing.

These kids feel like outsiders. They feel their person is despised. They were not star athletes or school leaders, but kids who are out of the mainstream, unhappy, searching for their place, and suffering ridicule. Full of rage, selfishness, and looking for thrills, they are the kids who kill their parents and others.

U.S. New and World Report, June 1, 1998, called one child from Springfield, Oregon, that went on a killing rampage "just a bad seed." He was from what appeared to be a good home where the parents were involved in the child's life. It is certain he was not a righteous seed. Something was wrong.

DISTURBED CHILDREN

What factors contribute to the lives of disturbed children?

I. *Millions of children are growing up without any real under-*

standing of love. A child cannot be normal without experiencing love. This is your first area of attack to turn them around. Learn to express love and bond with them. Babies are not the only ones who need to bond.

2. *The more sensitive the child, the deeper the needs and the more severe the problems.* Sensitivity can be a great blessing, but when it is allowed to fester in self-centeredness, it can be very destructive.

3. *Something terrible about our society is revealed when one of the groups committing suicide is five to eleven year old children.* We find children younger and younger deliberately hurting themselves.

4. *Many children are simply spoiled and determined to have their own way no matter what it costs those who love them.* They have not learned to value others nor have they been taught to respect and serve others. We must move them out of this total "self focus" to care about those around them.

5. *Drugs are a malignancy in the world today.* Heroin especially is a terrible addiction and the cause of suicide both deliberate and accidental among teenagers. Heroin use slacked off some but now it is making a comeback.

Young people get into drugs for different reasons. Some just do it for the fun, some just want to fit into the crowd, and some do drugs to escape their problems. Whatever the reason, few are really prepared for the addiction that follows. Children in this condition are delusional and irrational. Drugs render them incapable of truth, honor, or even respect for parents.

Tough love is usually recommended in such cases. In severe cases, some advise you to kick the child out, cut them off, do not let them come back home, and do not even answer the

PRESERVING A RIGHTEOUS SEED

phone. I suppose in some cases tough love becomes necessary, but I do not believe it is a blanket answer that covers all cases. Some who have taken this route say this is not a good solution and offers little comfort to the parents going through a child's addiction.

My advice is to do what you have to do. It is so easy to live in denial because we just do not want to face or admit it is true. But you must wake up so that you can be there for them. Refusing to face the problem gives no place for solution. Search their rooms, know what is there. I can hear some of you screaming already, "Invasion of privacy!"

The truth is that the protection of the privacy of teens under all circumstances is not love. A child who brings drugs and related trash into your home is out of control and has lost his or her right to privacy or any freedom from search and seizure. He or she is abusing the sanctity of your home.

Remember that your child is not in charge! You are! By your intervention, you encourage the formation of righteousness in your children. For the atmosphere of your home to be righteous, you must establish order in the early formative years of your children's lives.

Burn their pornography; do not throw it out where someone else may find it. I understand some of it is almost impossible to bum because of the paper it is printed on, but I urge you to destroy it somehow. Flush their drugs and get rid of bad music. Do this in a mature way, not as a frenzied, deranged, angry parent. Your children must know that you love them too much to allow their destruction in your home.

Don't make excuses for them or defend their guilt or overly protect them. If you discover your child is using drugs, do not push him or her out of the home unless you have done everything in your power to salvage the situation. And make sure that your child has a safe place to go. If you just cannot cope any longer or it is destroying your home and the other children in the home, then you must make the decision to act.

Pray and be wise. This is an important decision. When your child leaves your home without a godly place to go, he or she is thrust out into the arms of Satan. Unless you cover the child in prayer, Satan can take advantage of the situation. You may be turning your child over to the devil and losing the opportunity for future input in his or her life.

While you have the opportunity, work to establish an atmosphere of communication. Talk with your children, not *at* them. Hopefully you have already built a foundation of trust. Keep talking! They must know you care for *them,* not just your reputation or your pain. They need to learn to live in the light. You must know where they are spiritually and encourage them to expose the secret, hidden corners of their lives.

Never make threats you do not want to carry out. Many parents, especially mothers, make all kinds of outlandish threats they have no intention of going through with. This will cause your children to lose respect for you as a parent. Guard your tongue! Shut your mouth on everything negative and pray. God can do what you cannot do. Stand in the gap and fast. Fasting is an effective tool. Do not panic and act as if there is no God. God is still on His throne. There is always hope, no matter how bad things seem to you. Where there is life there is hope. We badly underestimate God. Nothing is impossible if we put our faith in God and walk before Him humbly and righteously.

6. The number one cause of death for American teens is drunk driving, and Christian kids are in on the party. Drinking, drugs, and oral sex are the "rage" of our teen culture. All three are potential killers. All three are symptoms of deep needs, peer pressure, and a lack of understanding and concern for the laws of God and the land.

Kids turn to drugs, alcohol, smoking, and overeating to hide emotional, spiritual, or physical pain. Some just become involved to appear cool or to find a measure of satisfaction and love they perceive as coming out of these four things.

Negative peer pressure is like the story about a bucket of crabs. There is no need to put a lid on the bucket because if one crab starts to crawl out the others will grab on to him and pull him back down. This is a good example of negative peer pressure.

7. *Depression among teens is common.* As I was writing this chapter, my husband came back from a two-week ministry trip to Iceland. He learned while there that Iceland is the number one country among the nations for teen suicides. The basic root of this problem seemed to be isolation.

Iceland's major industry is fishing. Seventy percent of its income comes from fishing. Many of the men are at sea for thirty to thirty-five days at a time, coming home exhausted from twelve-hour shifts, and with a brief stay of less than a week, they return for another month at sea. Women are left to cope alone and children see little of their fathers. Depression is extensive in the country.

8. *The children who develop anorexia and bulimia are usually very intelligent and very sensitive.* The injustice, pain, and violence in the world takes a toll on anorexics. These children are characterized by a lack of appetite or erratic eating patterns that control their lives. Generally, deep pain and rejection serve as a foundation for this problem. The image they have of themselves is severely distorted by their delusion that they are overweight. Depression, anxiety, and isolation overwhelm them.

9. *Autism affects some children.* Many young people afflicted with autism are near geniuses in one or more areas. My friend with a doctorate in this area believes, as I do, that pain experienced in the womb or shortly thereafter may cause portions of the personality to shut down in these children, rendering them unable to tolerate or cope with the ugliness and pain of the real world. Two characteristics of these disturbed children is complete self-absorption and reduced ability to respond or communicate with the outside world.

10. *Self injury and self mutilation are on the rise.* This horror is due to inner pain or "self-loathing." It is a destructive and perverted release from emotional pain. The aim of these children is to hurt themselves to gain attention or control. They often say, "I had control!" They use knives, razors, acid bums, safety pins, irons, oven cleaners, anything that will cause pain. This becomes an addiction but is rarely followed by suicide.

11. *An attachment disorder is another form of crisis facing children today.* We are being told that at least thirty percent of all children of foreign adoption are struggling with this problem. These are children who have never known love and see the world as a battleground.

Obviously there are American children who also suffer in this way. Full of anger and never having bonded to anyone, they are violent and disruptive, tearing apart families and destroying homes. Many of them were abused sexually and in other ways and many never recover. We have been close to a number of these cases. They are heart-wrenching and nearly impossible to live with.

Self-esteem is made up of two parts: self-confidence, the sense of being competent to function and produce in life and self-respect, the sense that one is worthy or worthwhile. These children have been robbed of both these important elements, and the very core of their being has been destroyed.

One family we know has a little European girl who suffers from this disorder. When they first got her as a tiny child, she would huddle in a corner in a fetal position saying, "I have no home, no one wants me." Now, at twelve years of age, in spite of a loving home and parents who try hard to meet her needs, she is a very difficult child. The bitterness still comes out in spite and rebellion, lying and misrepresenting her parents. She seems to have little conscience. It is a sad thing, but nothing is impossible for the Lord and her parents continue to pray.

WHAT TO DO?

It would be easy to throw up our hands and cop out. But we as parents must remember that life is responsibility. That means we may lose sleep, we may lose face, we may become weary and perplexed, but we must not bail out and push our children away because they are making life difficult for us. What can we do? We can face the facts, acknowledge the truth, refuse to operate in denial, make corrections, evaluate our position, refuse to make excuses, and act courageously.

This is not the easy road. It will cost. But there is cost either way, and it is better to suffer on the side of righteousness than to cop out and suffer with eternal results that leave your children outside the kingdom of God. Refuse to take the easy road!

DO children from good homes go astray? Yes, of course, we all know they do. Dysfunctional children can come from Bible believing, church-going homes, where the mother is at home for the children. It is not as likely, but it does happen.

What can you do to prevent these things from happening in your family? I want to emphasize again some of the important things we as parents can do to help our children come through these teenage years into maturity without "crashing and burning."

1. *Our children need our prayers.* It is the most important thing you can do. This should come from two godly parents who are in unity concerning their children. But any parent who walks before the Lord in righteousness can have a tremendous impact on the lives of their children. In the light of eternity, this is the deciding factor in a child's life. Without it, the formation of a righteous seed is very difficult. Are you growing, and molding righteous seed for God or are you just putting a roof over the heads of your children and letting them grow up on their own terms?

Many children today do not even know who God is. They think they are free to make the rules they live by. They try, if they have any concept of God, to use God to fulfill their plans. It is ironic to hear people on television acknowledging God, even while it is known that they are living in gross sin. No wonder our kids are confused. They need to know that the rules we live by can bring us peace and happiness or chaos and destruction.

2. *Our children need a Savior.* They need to know God as a Father to them; One who came to take their sins, their pain, and their insecurities. They need to know God is the healer of their poor self-image as well as their physical ills. They may never know and understand that fact unless you model it before them.

3. *Our children need to be touched.* I cannot express to you how tremendously important I feel this is for children and adults. So many people have never been bonded to anyone, not even their mothers. Without this ability to bond with others, they feel alone and become vulnerable to the devil.

My oldest son at the age of fourteen or fifteen was miserable. No one was showing him much love because he just did not seem to want love. The Lord finally pointed the problem out to me and I began a campaign to love this child aggressively. I would wrestle him, in a teasing way, to the floor and kiss him over and over. I did this every day for a while and before I realized it, he began to come into the kitchen and get his hugs and love. Today, he is a loving person, a pastor who loves his people.

Learn to gently touch others in a pure way. I realize there are inappropriate ways to touch, but our society is suffering because we are afraid to touch others at all even with purity of heart.

Parents who push their children away, scream at them, and verbally abuse them, should not be surprised to find themselves rejected someday. Children, because of their needs, will forgive a lot, but there is a point beyond which they become bitter and unforgiving. You nor they know where that point is. Give them loving discipline, unfailing love, and very quick forgiveness.

In ministering with my husband, I often open my arms and take women in "bear hugs." I lock my hands behind their backs and just hold them tight. They sometimes tell me, "I don't ever remember my mother or parents hugging me." They usually do not want to turn me loose. There is such a need in people, young and old, for the touch of other human beings.

There is great encouragement in that most kids find a way through or around these problems. Again, it is hard to tell which children will find their way around and which ones will become disturbed.

4. *Our children need to work consistently without expectation of reward.* They need to know being rewarded for work is good but giving their work in community and as a servant of God is good as well. Children who are given too much and have never

learned to work, demand everything and give little of themselves in return. Much of this is our fault as parents. Children who have been given too much can cause other children to feel deprived and cheated.

5. *Our children learn to communicate by communicating with us.* Not only do children need to connect physically with those around them, but they need to learn to communicate with others. As parents, we must set a good example for them. We cannot do that by talking down to them or rudely ordering them around. We would not talk to friends the way we talk to our children sometimes.

When you speak to your children, be sure you show them that you respect and appreciate them as human beings. All children need the input of family to keep them straight. Keep the lines of communication open.

RESOURCE SUGGESTIONS

Michael and Debi Pearl, To Train Up A Child, 100 Pearl Rd., Pleasantville, TN, 37147, USA, 1994, (I highly recommend this book).

Elisa Morgan and Carol Kuykendall, What Every Child Needs, This is a publication of MOPS (Mothers of Preschoolers Int.).

James R. Lucas, Pro Active Parenting. Harvest House Publishers, Eugene, Oregon, 97402, 1993.

David Jeremiah, Exposing the Myths of Parenthood, Word Publishing, 1501 LBJ Freeway, Dallas, TX, 75234, 1988.

H. Norman Wright, Family Is Still A Great Idea, Servant Publications, Ann Arbor, Michigan, 1992.

Larry Anderson, Taking Trauma Out of Teen Transition, Navpress, P.O. Box 35001, Colorado Springs, CO, 30935, 1991.

Carolyn Johnson, Forever a Parent, Zondervan Publishing House, Grand Rapids, Ml, 1992, (This book deals with adult children).

Lynda Hunter, Parenting On Your Own, Crossings, P.O. Box 6336, Indianapolis, IN, 46206-6336.

Mark Hanby with Craig Lindsay Ervin, You Have Not Many Fathers, Destiny Image, P.O. Box 310, Shippensburg, PA, 17257, 1996.

Henry Cloud and John Townsend, Boundaries With Kids, Zondervan Publishing House, Grand Rapids, ML

James Dobson, <u>Dr. James Dobson on Parenting,</u> Inspiration Press.

Adrien Rogers, <u>Perfect 10 Series,</u> Love Worth Finding Ministries,
P.O. Box 38-800, Memphis, TN, 38183.

James Robison, <u>God Centered Parenting,</u> Phone 1-800-947-LIFE (5433).

Bill Gothard, <u>Institute in Basic Life Principles,</u> Box 1, Oak Brook, IL. 60522-3001.

PRESERVING A RIGHTEOUS SEED

About the Author

Joyce Thompson has been married for thirty-eight years and is the mother of four sons and two daughters. She has served as a pastor's wife and a missionary to Brazil, Portugal, and Australia. She has a B.S. in education with minors in English and bible and graduate work in religious education.

Her husband, Carrol Thompson, is a graduate of Southwestern Baptist Theological Seminary in Ft. Worth, Texas. He has been in full-time ministry for forty-five years. He is a preacher of righteousness and a deliverance teacher who lives what he teaches.

www.ingramcontent.com/pod-product-compliance
Lightning Source LLC
Chambersburg PA
CBHW071519040426
42444CB00008B/1725